First World War
and Army of Occupation
War Diary
France, Belgium and Germany

52 DIVISION
Divisional Troops
Royal Army Medical Corps
1/2 Lowland Field Ambulance
17 April 1918 - 31 May 1919

WO95/2894/2

The Naval & Military Press Ltd
www.nmarchive.com
Published in association with The National Archives

Published by

The Naval & Military Press Ltd

Unit 10 Ridgewood Industrial Park,

Uckfield, East Sussex,

TN22 5QE England

Tel: +44 (0) 1825 749494

www.naval-military-press.com

www.nmarchive.com

This diary has been reprinted in facsimile from the original. Any imperfections are inevitably reproduced and the quality may fall short of modern type and cartographic standards.

© Crown Copyright
Images reproduced by permission of The National Archives, London, England, 2015.

Contents

Document type	Place/Title	Date From	Date To
Heading	WO95/2894-2		
Heading	52nd Division 1/2nd (Lowland) Fld Ambnce Apr 1918-1919 May		
Heading	War Diary of For Period 1st April 1918 to 30th April 1918 Vol 1		
War Diary	Marseilles.	17/04/1918	19/04/1918
War Diary	In The Train. France	20/04/1918	21/04/1918
War Diary	Noyelles.	22/04/1918	22/04/1918
War Diary	Estreboeuf	23/04/1918	29/04/1918
War Diary	La Lacque	30/04/1918	30/04/1918
Heading	War Diary of For Period 1/5/18 to 31/5/18 Vol 2		
War Diary	La Lacque	01/05/1918	05/05/1918
War Diary	Aux Rietz	06/05/1918	25/05/1918
War Diary	St Eloi	25/05/1918	31/05/1918
Miscellaneous	Arrangement for evacuation from Man Battle Station Lys Canal Area Appendix I		
Miscellaneous	Appendix II		
War Diary	Aux Rietz	13/05/1918	13/05/1918
Heading	War Diary of From 1/6/18 to 30/6/18 Vol 3		
War Diary	Mont St Eloi	01/06/1918	18/06/1918
War Diary	4 Vents	18/06/1918	30/06/1918
War Diary	War Diary of July 1918 Vol 4		
War Diary	Lesquatre Vent W.9 Central Sheet 44B.	01/06/1918	05/06/1918
War Diary	Les 4 Vents	06/06/1918	21/06/1918
War Diary	Auchel	22/07/1918	30/07/1918
War Diary	Barlin	31/07/1918	31/07/1918
Miscellaneous	To oi\c W.W.C.P. Appx I		
Miscellaneous	Amended Batt and Treatment Summary		
Miscellaneous	Routine to be adopted in (VIII) Corps Skin Centre for Scabies. App. III.		
Miscellaneous	The Role of The 1/2 Nd Low. Fd. Ambce. In The Medical Arrangements of The 52nd Division Are As Follows. Appx. II	16/07/1918	16/07/1918
Heading	War Diary 1/2nd Lowland Field Ambce RAMC (T) From 1st Augt 1918 to 31st Augt 1918 Vol 5		
War Diary	Maroeuil	01/08/1918	17/08/1918
War Diary	Gouy-Servins	18/08/1918	20/08/1918
War Diary	Duisans Sheet 51C (Loc 46)	21/08/1918	22/08/1918
War Diary	Bretencourt	23/08/1918	23/08/1918
War Diary	Ficheux	24/08/1918	24/08/1918
War Diary	S 11 C 29 (Sheet 51B)	25/08/1918	25/08/1918
War Diary	Boiry Becquerelle	26/08/1918	26/08/1918
War Diary	In The Field	27/08/1918	27/08/1918
War Diary	Mercatel	28/08/1918	31/08/1918
Diagram etc	Store Appx. I.		
Miscellaneous	Total Battle Casualties on Western Front From 17-4-18 to 28-8-18 Appendix VII	00/08/1918	00/08/1918
Diagram etc	Underground Dressing Station.		
Diagram etc	Diagram of Routes of Evacuation 2nd August 1918 Appx III		

Miscellaneous	Appendix to 157 Inf Bde. Defence Scheme Evacuation Of Sick And Wounded Appx IV	05/08/1918	05/08/1918
Miscellaneous	Evacuations from ADS to Corps M.D.S. from 6 pm on 23rd aug to 12 noon on 25th August Appendix V		
Miscellaneous	Appendix VI		
Heading	War Diary for September 1918 2nd Lowland F.A. Vol 6		
War Diary	Croisilles. Sheet 51 B.	01/09/1918	03/09/1918
War Diary	Queant	04/09/1918	04/09/1918
War Diary	Noreuil C 10 C 9.1.	05/09/1918	06/09/1918
War Diary	U.25.a.2.0	07/09/1918	12/09/1918
War Diary	U 25a 20 (Sheet 51 C)	13/09/1918	16/09/1918
War Diary	U.9. Central Sheet 57 C	17/09/1918	19/09/1918
War Diary	C 9 Central	20/09/1918	25/09/1918
War Diary	C 9 Central (57 C)	26/09/1918	26/09/1918
War Diary	Beet Root Factory J.9b 4.1 (Sheet 57 C)	27/09/1918	27/09/1918
War Diary	J 9b 4.1	28/09/1918	30/09/1918
Miscellaneous	ADMS 52nd Division	12/09/1918	12/09/1918
Miscellaneous			
Miscellaneous	Contents of Battle A.D.S. Limbered Wagon App I		
Heading	War Diary for October 1918 1/2nd Lowland Field Ambulance Vol 7		
War Diary	Sheet 57.C. J.9.b.5.4	01/10/1918	01/10/1918
War Diary	Sheet 57 C. F25 a.3.5 Anneux	02/10/1918	04/10/1918
War Diary	Anneux	05/10/1918	06/10/1918
War Diary	J.9.b 4.2 (Doignies)	07/10/1918	16/10/1918
War Diary	Blavincourt	17/10/1918	18/10/1918
War Diary	St Eloy.	19/10/1918	19/10/1918
War Diary	Henin Lietard P.25. Sheet 44. A.	20/10/1918	20/10/1918
War Diary	Henin Lietard	21/10/1918	23/10/1918
War Diary	Flines-Lez-Raches (R 23 Sheet 44 A)	24/10/1918	24/10/1918
War Diary	Flines	25/10/1918	26/10/1918
War Diary	Landas	27/10/1918	27/10/1918
War Diary	Lecelles	28/10/1918	31/10/1918
Miscellaneous	Summary of Casualties Passed thro. A.D.S. 6 p.m. 1/10/18 to 6 am 2/10/18		
Miscellaneous	6 pm 2/10/18 to 6 am 3/10/18 Wounded Passed Sick		
Miscellaneous	From 6 A.M. on 4/10/18 to 6 A.M. on 5/10/18		
Heading	War Diary November 1918 1/2nd Low. Fld. Ambce. Vol 8		
War Diary	Lecelles I. 29 (Sheet 44)	01/11/1918	08/11/1918
War Diary	Hauterive J36 a.0.9 Sheet 44	09/11/1918	09/11/1918
War Diary	Grand Bruyere G9d 9 1	10/11/1918	11/11/1918
War Diary	Vacresse C.30 C 6.4 Sheet 45	12/11/1918	13/11/1918
War Diary	Erbisoeul	14/11/1918	30/11/1918
Heading	War Diary of from 1st Decr 1918 to 31st Decr 1918 Volume No. 43		
War Diary	Mon Railway Station	01/12/1918	31/12/1918
Heading	War Diary of From 1st Jany. to Jany 1919 1/2nd Lowland F.A. Volume No. 44		
War Diary	Mon Rly. Station	01/01/1919	31/01/1919
Heading	War Diary for Month of February 1919 1/2nd Lowland F.A. Volume 45		
War Diary	Mons Rly. Station	01/02/1919	28/02/1919
Miscellaneous	Organization of XXII Corps Halte Repas at Mons.		

Heading	1/2 Lowland Fa Amb War Diary for the month of March 1919 Vol 46		
War Diary	Mons Rly Station	01/03/1919	21/03/1919
War Diary	Soignies	22/03/1919	31/03/1919
Heading			
Heading	1/2nd Lowland F.A. Apr. 1919		
War Diary	Soignies	01/04/1919	30/04/1919
Heading	140/3660 1/2nd Lowland Field Ambulance. May 1919		
War Diary	Soignies	01/05/1919	31/05/1919

WO95/2894
(2)

52ND DIVISION

1/2ND (LOWLAND) FLD AMBNCE

APR 1918-~~DEC 1918~~ 1919 MAY

Army Form C. 2118.

WAR DIARY
or
INTELLIGENCE SUMMARY.

2nd L. F. AMBULANCE
R. A. M. CORPS (T).

(Erase heading not required.)

Instructions regarding War Diaries and Intelligence Summaries are contained in F. S. Regs., Part II. and the Staff Manual respectively. Title pages will be prepared in manuscript.

Place	Date	Hour	Summary of Events and Information	Remarks and references to Appendices

CONFIDENTIAL

WAR DIARY

OF

2nd L. F. AMBULANCE
R. A. M. CORPS (T).

FOR PERIOD:

1st April 1918 to 30th April 1918.

Vol I

140/2900

A. Cumming
Lieut. Col.
O.C. 2nd. Low. Fd. Ambce.
R. A. M. CORPS. T.

COMMITTEE FOR THE
MEDICAL HISTORY OF THE WAR

Date -6 JUN. 1918

(A7094). Wt W12839/M1293. 75,0 o. 1/17. D. D. & L., Ltd. Forms/C.2118/14.

MARSEILLES.	17/4/18	Arrived Marseilles Harbour 0830. 15 Patients transferred to Gen. Hosp. Marseilles. Disembarked 1100. & marched to No 10 Rest Camp. Party left to unload baggage. (M)
	18/4/18	Still at No 10 Rest Camp. Passes to town given to 10% of unit. I received intimation that I had been awarded the D.S.O. for services rendered in Palestine. (M)
	19/4/18	Capt Angus rejoined unit from leave to U.K. Baggage removed from Docks to Marseilles Military Station In accordance with instructions the unit left No 10 Rest Camp at 2100 & entrained at Marseilles Military Station. From State:- O. Officer 241 O.R. (M)

Army Form C. 2118.

WAR DIARY
or
INTELLIGENCE SUMMARY.
(Erase heading not required.)

Instructions regarding War Diaries and Intelligence Summaries are contained in F. S. Regs., Part II. and the Staff Manual respectively. Title pages will be prepared in manuscript.

Place	Date	Hour	Summary of Events and Information	Remarks and references to Appendices
IN THE TRAIN FRANCE	20/4/15		Left Marseille station 0920	
	21/4/15		Arrived Fp. del. 1430. Rations served & tea served. Arrived at Pony-le-Moniel 0730. Rations served & tea provided. Arrived at Moteher-leva 1900. Tea provided.	(1)
NOYELLES	22/4/15		Arrived at Noyelles & detrained at 1030. Camped overnight on encampment to West of Village.	(1)
ESTREBOEUF	23/4/15		Left Noyelles at 0730 & marched to Estreboeuf. Instructions to billet in Estreboeuf but on arrival found 9 Coy & H.Q.J. in occupation & same managed to obtain quarters at Francourt. Headquarters in Francourt Chateau, belonging to General Rodeguel. Marching in state - 8 officers & 192 OR RAMC - 48 OR RASC	(1)
	24/4/15		Received instructions from ADMS that all Cameras in possession of personnel of unit to be packed & sent to 2 H.Q. to be returned to U.K. After considerable trouble & delay managed to get the Postal Authorities to accept same for postage, but only on furnishing a certificate in respect of each parcel that as to the contents & the authority for their return.	(1)

Army Form C. 2118.

WAR DIARY
or
INTELLIGENCE SUMMARY.
(Erase heading not required.)

Instructions regarding War Diaries and Intelligence Summaries are contained in F. S. Regs., Part II. and the Staff Manual respectively. Title pages will be prepared in manuscript.

Place	Date	Hour	Summary of Events and Information	Remarks and references to Appendices
ESTREBOEUF	24/4/18		A second blanket was issued to personnel of unit. Capt. Roome in charge of transport then proceeded to the East Horse Transport Depôt returning at 1700 with our establishment of Transport Vehicles & 33 Horses	(A)
	25/4/18		Wrote ADMS re the return of 1 NCO & 1 O.R. of this unit attached to Hdqrs barrel-party. These men were useful men in this unit, each one was employed on special regimental duties & as greatly missed. Difficulty experienced in obtaining Motor Ambulances for the evacuation of sick to Abbeville.	(A)
	26/4/18		Wrote ADMS re the return of Lt. Morton M.O. 6th Hy. I. to this unit, to be replaced by Lt. Rotalough. Wrote ADMS re U/- & Q.M. Saddler of this unit who has not yet returned from leave to U.K. this unit has been operating without a Quarter-Master since 15/2/18. Application by Major Burns for a command, forwarded to ADMS.	(A) (A)
	27/4/18		Surplus Officers Kits returned to Base for U.K.	(A)

Army Form C. 2118.

WAR DIARY
or
INTELLIGENCE SUMMARY.
(Erase heading not required.)

Instructions regarding War Diaries and Intelligence Summaries are contained in F. S. Regs., Part II. and the Staff Manual respectively. Title pages will be prepared in manuscript.

Place	Date	Hour	Summary of Events and Information	Remarks and references to Appendices
ESTRÉE BOEUF	29/4/18		Received 8 Riding Horses - 5 Officers 3 Transport NCOs. Orders re move of Unit by rail postponed 24 hours. Whilst training of personnel in use & practice of wearing S.B. Respirator with Anti Gas No.1. the unit left Drancourt at	(W)
	22/4/18		In accordance with Adm Inst. No 1. the unit left Drancourt at 1200 & marched to NOYELLES Station for entrainment. Vehicles & Horses loaded, train moved off 9.20	(W)
LA LACQUE	23/4/18		Arrived BERGUETTE Station at 0500. A & C sections marched to La Lacque. Hutments leaving B section & transport personnel to unload the vehicles & horses. B section & transport arrived 0500. This move now transfers the 53rd Divn from general reserve to First Army, XI Corps. 4 Motor Ambulance Cars were attached to the Unit for duty. On request from ADMS list of MOs & 157th Bde shewing date of last leave to U.K. was submitted. Out of 12 Officers, 9 have had no leave since date of embarkation for service overseas, 3 of whom have been abroad practically 3 years.	(W)

Army Form C. 2118.

WAR DIARY
or
INTELLIGENCE SUMMARY.
(Erase heading not required.)

Vol 36

2nd L. F. AMBULANCE
R.A.M. CORPS (T.)

Vol 2.
140/2983

COMMITTEE FOR THE
MEDICAL HISTORY OF THE WAR
3 JUL 1918

CONFIDENTIAL

WAR DIARY
of
2nd L. F. AMBULANCE
R.A.M. CORPS (T.)
for period
1/5/18 to 31/5/18

W.A. Burns Major
o/c 2nd L. F. AMBULANCE
R.A.M. CORPS (T.)

Instructions regarding War Diaries and Intelligence Summaries are contained in F. S. Regs., Part II. and the Staff Manual respectively. Title pages will be prepared in manuscript.

Place	Date	Hour	Summary of Events and Information	Remarks and references to Appendices

Army Form C. 2118.

WAR DIARY
or
INTELLIGENCE SUMMARY.

2nd L.F. AMBULANCE
R.A.M. CORPS (T.)

(Erase heading not required.)

VOL 36

Place	Date	Hour	Summary of Events and Information	Remarks and references to Appendices
LA LACQUE	1/5/18		Lt. Riddough was detached as MO to A.T.S. to relieve Lt. Morton who returned to this unit for duty. ADMS visited camp today. A hospital was opened for the reception & treatment of sick of the Brigade. 2 Motor Cyclos were received. Two men of this unit with a knowledge of Motor Cyclos were detailed as despatch riders.	
	2/5/18		Orders received in connection with the manning of Battle Stations in the event of an attack by the enemy. 157th Brigade to occupy the BUSNES - STEENBECQUE Line from COURANT BRAYELLE River at Pt. C.H.7. to Southern edge of BOIS D'AMANT. 750. d.2.2. & also to place nucleus garrisons to hold all bridges over the LYS Canal from Pt Central to Pt. Central in connection with these arrangements I visited the area & selected sites for Collecting Stations & Advanced Dressing Station as per Appendix 2. (copy of arrangements for evacuations submitted to ADMS) A return shewing length of service abroad, without leave to UK, of personnel of this unit was submitted to ADMS. Over 3 years - 5. Over 2 years - 199. Over 1 year - 29.	

Army Form C. 2118.

WAR DIARY
or
INTELLIGENCE SUMMARY.
(Erase heading not required.)

2nd L. F. AMBULANCE
R.A.M. CORPS (T).

Place	Date	Hour	Summary of Events and Information	Remarks and references to Appendices
LA LACQUE	3/5/18		Capt. Rooms was detailed as M.O. to 52nd Gun Machine Gun Bat'n. Received Order S.R.9. Warning that 52nd Div. less RA will be transferred to 18th Corps by tactical trains on 6th 7th & 8th May and will complete the relief of 4th Canadian Division on night of 8th May.	
	4/5/18		2 Officers 10 O.R. accompanied Brigade to go through Gas School at MAMETZ. Wrote A.D.M.S. applying for my rank as Lieut. Col. to be substantiated.	
	5/5/18		In accordance with Brigade Adm shot No.8. the Transport less of this unit left at 10.00 to join Brigade transport at Pendeyeres (junction S of AIRE on AIRE – ST HILAIRE Road at 1130.) to proceed to MERICOURT sector of line. Transport moved by route march in two stages – May 5th from AIRE Area to DIVION. where they halted for the night – May 6th - from Divion to NEUVILLE ST VAAST. Lt. Norton took charge of transport of this unit. All baggage, equipment, etc were sent with transport. Capt. Lolole & 1 O.R. left to proceed with Brigade Billeting parties to NEUVILLE ST. VAAST at 10.00. 1 Officer 30 O.R. left to go through Gas at Gas School MAMETZ. Wrote A.D.M.S. asking for plan & disposition of Canadian Field Ambulances which this unit were proceeding to relieve.	

Army Form C. 2118.

WAR DIARY
or
INTELLIGENCE SUMMARY.
(Erase heading not required.)

2nd L. F. AMBULANCE
R. A. M. CORPS (T).

Place	Date	Hour	Summary of Events and Information	Remarks and references to Appendices
Aux Rietz	6/5/18		In accordance with orders the 154th Inf. Bde Order No 97. Mr Bregeot commenced entraining at AIRE to proceed to the MERICOURT SECTOR of the line to relieve the 11th Canadian Bde of 4th Canadian Divn on the line from T.23.C.6.0.6. Northern boundary of 4th Canadian Divn at T.3.6.4.0. 155th Bde to be in reserve at 97.ELOY arriving by tactical train on 7th inst. 156th Bde to be in support in NEUVILLE ST VAAST arriving by tactical train on 8th. In accordance with above Bde Orders, RAMC Operating Orders No1. this unit left LA LACQUE Camp at 0800, & proceeded to entrain at AIRE arriving off at 1015. On arrival at detraining Station MAROEUIL at 1356. I reported to ADMS 1st Canadian Divn at Aux Rietz and received instructions re the relief of 12th Canadian Field Ambce at Aux RIETZ. A.S.C.	
	7/5/18		The unit proceeded to Aux RIETZ & to be billeted for the night. Immediately on arrival 2 Officers & 40 O.R. were despatched to the Advanced Dressing Stn at LA CHAUDIERE & 2 Off. HO O.R. to ADSn at VIMY VILLAGE in order that they might become familiar with the Relay posts & RAP before taking over from the Canadian Field Ambce at 1800 on 7th inst. 2 Motor Ambulance Cars reported from 136th Field Ambce. The relief of the 12th Canadian Field Ambce was carried out, the Main Dressing Station, 2 Advance Dressing Station & all evacuating posts being taken over at 1180	

Army Form C. 2118.

2nd L. F. AMBULANCE
R. A. M. CORPS (T).

WAR DIARY
or
INTELLIGENCE SUMMARY.
(Erase heading not required.)

Instructions regarding War Diaries and Intelligence Summaries are contained in F. S. Regs., Part II. and the Staff Manual respectively. Title pages will be prepared in manuscript.

Place	Date	Hour	Summary of Events and Information	Remarks and references to Appendices
AUX RIETZ	7/5/18.		The Main Dressing Station consists of Hutments with Electric light Installation and Large & Deep dugouts which afford admirable protection for personnel.	
			All area stores. 433 Blankets. 116 Stretchers & 13 Thomas Splints were taken over.	
			6 Motor Ambulance Cars of 8th M.A.C. were attached to Main Dressing Station for evacuation of patients from there.	
			Evacuations are carried out by Motor Ambulance from A.D.M.S, (two cars being stationed at each A.D.S for this purpose) to M.D. Stn. & by cars of 8th M.A.C to the group of CCSs. at AUBIGNY, or other hospital for special cases as detailed on DDMS instructions No 2934/4 (Summary of Medical arrangements of XVIII Corps).	
	8/5/18.		Wrote A.D.M.S. re the supply of soda Breast which had been indented for a week ago & has not yet been received. This is urgently required for the treatment of gassed cases in the event of an enemy gas attack. Repeated demands from R.M.Os are arriving which cannot be supplied.	
			Wrote A.D.M.S re return of Deficiencies in Ordnance Equipment which had been submitted for over consecutive days without result.	
			Reported to A.D.M.S. my arrangements for evacuation of patients from R.A.Ps. as per Appendix D attached	

Army Form C. 2118.

2nd L. F. AMBULANCE
R. A. M. CORPS (T).

WAR DIARY
or
INTELLIGENCE SUMMARY.
(Erase heading not required.)

Place	Date	Hour	Summary of Events and Information	Remarks and references to Appendices
Aux RIETZ	9/8/18		Received information that a German offensive was expected soon probably tonight between 10.30 pm & 1.30 am if not tonight it may take place the following night. As a precautionary movement all our transport wagons horses & stores not at present in use were despatched to VILLERS-AU-BOIS to be stationed there. Arrangements were made with O.C. of the Light Railway which runs past the M.D. Stn to SAVY for the speedy evacuation of patients in the event of an influx of wounded. Wrote British Red Cross Socy asking for 12 Distinguishing Boxes for use at the Adv Dressing Station, Relay posts & RAPs these could not be supplied by B.R.C. so they an improvised Distinguishing Boxes were made from Biscuit tins & supplied to the various posts. Notified O.C. Sections to detail runners to keep in touch with BHQ in order that immediate notice could be had in the event of a proposed change of location. O.C. Sections were also notified to warn all NCOs & men against taking orders from unknown persons. 315963 Pte Gibson H one of the stretcher bearers at CHAUDIERE was slightly wounded. The DDMS and ADMS visited the A.D. Stn Vimy.	

Army Form C. 2118.

WAR DIARY
or
INTELLIGENCE SUMMARY.
(Erase heading not required.)

2nd L. F. AMBULANCE
R. A. M. CORPS (T).

Place	Date	Hour	Summary of Events and Information	Remarks and references to Appendices
AUX RIETZ.	10/5/18		I visited the Adv. Dressing Station & inspected the post & evacuating channel. Stopped by ADMS. that Officers Leave for this Division had now opened and the allotment to this unit was now W.O.R. for 13 men. In reply to request by ADMS. for particulars as to arrangement with O.C. Light Railway for evacuation of patients. I stated that the journey to SAVY takes 3 hours. 20 sitting cases can be accommodated in one truck. Train consists of 5 trucks – 12 stretcher cases can be taken in a truck. Received DDMS instructions No. 999 – Summary of Medical Arrangements of XVIII Corps in the event of a hostile attack. In accordance with instructions received from ADMS (S.R.42 dd 10/5/18) an Amble bar Relay Post was established at Tilloch cross roads. (A.11.a.9.9.)	
	11/5/18		Received S.R. 45 instructions to be carried out in the event of a gas attack. All gassed cases to be admitted to this unit. Wrote ADMS. asking if Wheeled stretcher Carriages could be supplied, to assist the bearers in evacuating casualties.	

Army Form C. 2118.

2nd L.F. AMBULANCE
R.A.M. CORPS (T).

WAR DIARY
or
INTELLIGENCE SUMMARY.
(Erase heading not required.)

Instructions regarding War Diaries and Intelligence Summaries are contained in F. S. Regs., Part II. and the Staff Manual respectively. Title pages will be prepared in manuscript.

Place	Date	Hour	Summary of Events and Information	Remarks and references to Appendices
AUX RIETZ	11/5/18		Wrote ADMS asking if anything had been done with regard to my application on the 4th inst with reference to my substantive rank. Reply to effect that nothing had been done, as yet.	
			Forwarded instructions to O.C. B & C Sections regarding the clerical arrangements at their Stations & the use of A.F.W 3210 & Field Medical Cards.	
			As instructed by ADMS 6 tents were pitched to provide accommodation for patients in the event of an influx.	
			Notified by ADMS that Horse transport should be used for the removal of sick within the Dumesnil area, instead of motor Ambulance cars.	
			As instructed by ADMS 1 O.R. of this unit was detailed to report to O/C Baths Berthonval Farm for the purpose of working the Foden Disinfector there.	
	12/5/18		Major Boyd RAMC arrived & instructed as to the method adopted by 10th Field Ambces in the Laser sector on the forward area the Major Burns proceeded to the A.D.Stns & made a tour of the evacuation route. Nothing of material importance was learned.	

Army Form C. 2118.

WAR DIARY
or
INTELLIGENCE SUMMARY.
(Erase heading not required.)

2nd L. F. AMBULANCE
R. A. M. CORPS (T).

Instructions regarding War Diaries and Intelligence Summaries are contained in F. S. Regs., Part II. and the Staff Manual respectively. Title pages will be prepared in manuscript.

Place	Date	Hour	Summary of Events and Information	Remarks and references to Appendices
AUX RIETZ	19/5/18		Wrote ADMS re. 21 Thomas Uphints ancestors. Gave, which had been indented for on 7th inst. had not yet been received & Motor limber Cars were returned to OC 5th MAC as per ADMS instructions. As instructed by ADMS dressing teams were made to assist walking wounded on the evacuating route. Many observations are being received here from the relatives of men of the unit asking what leave cannot be granted, although leave has now been granted to this unit the allotment is so small that it will take 2 months to exhaust the personnel. Wrote ADMS about my absentation for home leave submitted on 26th inst. This is my 5th application for leave & WR all of which have been refused on the grounds that no MOs can be spared.	
	1/25/18		Wrote ADMS asking if anything could be done to construct a safer Dressing Station than that which at present exists at VIMY. The present one is but part of ruins of dwellings & is subjected to daily shelling from the enemy	

Army Form C. 2118.

2nd L. F. AMBULANCE.
R.A.M. CORPS (T).

WAR DIARY
or
INTELLIGENCE SUMMARY.
(Erase heading not required.)

Instructions regarding War Diaries and Intelligence Summaries are contained in F. S. Regs., Part II. and the Staff Manual respectively. Title pages will be prepared in manuscript.

Place	Date	Hour	Summary of Events and Information	Remarks and references to Appendices
Nv RUTZ.	13/5/18		Wrote ADMS with reference to recent instructions issued by him, asking if the stretcher bearers of the 1/5 L.F.A. as detailed in his instructions could be sent forward to the Advanced Dressing Stns in order to become familiar with the evacuating routes. Made further arrangements for evacuation of patients by rail as per APPENDIX IV (Correspondence with OC Light Railway.) As instructed by ADMS the 4 acres of land around the MDS in cultivated by the present occupants of this stn received further attention. The 3rd Canadian Divisional Agricultural officer called & advised as to the further cultivation of this land. A party of men from my station are busy duly attending to the acres allotted to this unit. 47 Gloves Hedging of 2/2 Gloves bottom unit two were received from personnel trenching gas casualties. Notified by ADMS to have a reconnaissance made with a view to having a Relay Post established in order to evacuate from an R.A.P. of 5th KOSB (B.13.a.8.8.) (worked on being evacuated via 5/1st Divn) to VIMY ADS. Replied as per APPENDIX III	

Army Form C. 2118.

2nd L.F. AMBULANCE
R.A.M. CORPS (T).

WAR DIARY
or
INTELLIGENCE SUMMARY.
(Erase heading not required.)

Place	Date	Hour	Summary of Events and Information	Remarks and references to Appendices
AUX RIETZ	13/5/18		After I had visited the R.A.P as mentioned above, S/M Millar & 4 bearers were despatched at 1900 to report to R.M.O 5th K.O.S.B. that 4 bearers were posted there to assist in the evacuation of patients with the Regt Major returned. Received notification the following day that evacuation of this post would be carried out over 51st Div by means of their bearers posted there.	
	14/5/18		Got bearer party 4 O.R. proceeded to Boulogne en route to U.K. Wrote ADMS about Methylated spirits which had been indented for 4 days ago now urgently required, but not yet received. Wrote B.R.A. from whom I received a letter stating that practically nothing of whom I had intended for could be supplied, explaining that in Egypt no difficulty was ever experienced in obtaining necessaries which could not be obtained from any other source.	
	15/5/18		As instructed by ADMS one extra days rations were drawn & had in reserve. O/c 156th Inf Bde relieved the 155th Inf Bde in the R. sector of the Divnl Line tonight. 1 N.C.O & 20 bearers from 1/3 W.L.A. reported & in accordance with ADMS	

Army Form C. 2118.

WAR DIARY
or
INTELLIGENCE SUMMARY.
(Erase heading not required.)

2nd L.F. AMBULANCE
R.A.M. CORPS (T).

Instructions regarding War Diaries and Intelligence Summaries are contained in F.S. Regs., Part II. and the Staff Manual respectively. Title pages will be prepared in manuscript.

Place	Date	Hour	Summary of Events and Information	Remarks and references to Appendices
AUX RIETZ	10/5/18	contd	instructions were despatched at once in parties to the Adv. Dressing Stns in order to become familiar with the evacuating routes.	
			Difficulty is experienced in obtaining stationary in spite of repeated demands for books & forms urgently required.	
			In accordance with ADM's instructions 1 NCO & 1 OR which were recruits to the establishment of this unit were sent to report to ADM's 50th Divn for refooting.	
			So many ambiguous orders are being received here especially with regard to evacuation that it is extremely difficult to know the exact procedure of evacuation to follow.	
			Wrote ADMS, re. the discontented feeling existing amongst my officers with regard to leave to U.K.	
	16/5/18		Subscriptions by this unit amounting to £13 francs were forwarded to ADMS in aid of erection of 59nd Divnl Memorial in Egypt.	
			1 officer & 4 OR (MT) ASC reported this now complete our establishment of (MT) ASC personnel.	
			ADMS & myself visited A.D.S. VIMY in the morning	

Army Form C. 2118.

2nd L. F. AMBULANCE
R.A.M. CORPS (T.)

WAR DIARY
or
INTELLIGENCE SUMMARY.
(Erase heading not required.)

Instructions regarding War Diaries and Intelligence Summaries are contained in F. S. Regs., Part II. and the Staff Manual respectively. Title pages will be prepared in manuscript.

Place	Date	Hour	Summary of Events and Information	Remarks and references to Appendices
AUX RIETZ	14/5/18	Contd	Capt Angus Vanay was replaced by Lieut Morton	
			Wrote A.D.M.S. again about leave suggesting that my case be sent to Corps Commander.	
			Myself, Capt Golds, Capt Angus & Lt Morton attended a lecture given by the Consulting Surgeon 1st Army at 3 p.m. (at camp of 1/3 L.F.A.) on the application of the Thomas Splint, and at 4 p.m. attended a Gas Defence Lecture given by the Consulting Physician	
	17/5/18		40 O.R. "A" Sec. relieved "B" Section at the Adv. Dressing Stn Chandelier.	
			Lt Morton was detailed to report as M.O. 1/5 H.L.I. vice Lieut McKenzie evacuated sick.	
	18/5/18		Capt Mansfield reported in accordance with ADMS instructions from 1/3 L.F.A. & was despatched to A.D.S. Vanay.	
			1 N.C.O. & O.R. 1/3 L.F.A. arrived to relieve the party of that unit at present attached here.	
			Lt & Q.M. Liddell reported after being absent on leave to U.K. since 13th Feby. 1918.	

Army Form C. 2118.

2nd L. F. AMBULANCE
R. A. M. CORPS (T).

WAR DIARY
or
INTELLIGENCE SUMMARY.
(Erase heading not required.)

Place	Date	Hour	Summary of Events and Information	Remarks and references to Appendices
Aux Rietz	17/6/18		Notified O.C. Sisters to collect all salvage around their stations who to store daily & sent by rail to Salvage Dump. Capt Black & 3 O.R. proceeded to Boulogne en route for UK on 14 days leave. Major Barrow & Capt Kant attended lectures on the Thomas Splints & Gas defence given at ST ELOI today.	
	18/6/18		The DDMS visited horses accompanied by the ADMS inspected camp today & Thomas returned to ADS Onin whilst Capt Mansfield replaced him as MO 4/5 H.L.I. He instructed by ADMS 3 Cylinders Oxygen were received from 1/3 L.F.A. & 1 from 1/1st L.F.A. Wrote ADMS about 318296 Pte Borland R. who was employed as Tailor Sailor to this unit was taken away as costumier to 5? Gun Concert Party. He is a most useful man here & can not be replaced as there are no other trained tailors with this unit. Copy of War Diary for Dec 1917 sent to ADMS as original had been lost at Sea.	

Army Form C. 2118.

2nd L.F. AMBULANCE
R.A.M. CORPS (T).

WAR DIARY
or
INTELLIGENCE SUMMARY.
(Erase heading not required.)

Instructions regarding War Diaries and Intelligence Summaries are contained in F. S. Regs., Part II. and the Staff Manual respectively. Title pages will be prepared in manuscript.

Place	Date	Hour	Summary of Events and Information	Remarks and references to Appendices
AUX RIETZ	20/6/18		4 Wheeled stretcher carriers arrived and were sent up to the ADS Decauvy. Stns & dayvo stores were also received. On writing A.D.M.S asking if it is at all possible to have telephone communication from Bois Hydges in order to facilitate early evacuation from region of collecting zone. Reply received that this cannot be done with suggestion that the further telephone at ADS Signal office be used. The DMS, DDMS & ADMS visited camp today. They also visited the ADS Vimy. About 5 minutes after they had left the station it was deliberately shelled but fortunately no damage was done. An artillery officer who had observed the shelling volunteered the opinion that the attack was deliberate & that it was the result of minimal amount of movement about the camp yesterday which are under direct enemy observation.	
	21/6/18		With reference to notification (SR63) from ADMS re the withdrawal of troops in the event of a gas attack & the request for new bearers chosen for AD Stn in conformity with movements of troops. Reported as per Appendix V.	

Army Form C. 2118.

2nd L. F. AMBULANCE
R. A. M. CORPS (T).

WAR DIARY
or
INTELLIGENCE SUMMARY.
(Erase heading not required.)

Instructions regarding War Diaries and Intelligence Summaries are contained in F. S. Regs., Part II. and the Staff Manual respectively. Title pages will be prepared in manuscript.

Place	Date	Hour	Summary of Events and Information	Remarks and references to Appendices
Aux Rietz	22/5/18		Wrote ADMS with reference to the authorised nos. of French stretchers of 36 per Fld Amb. Asking if these could be obtained. 4 Talbot cars & our establishment of MT personnel arrived today from 52nd Divn MT Coy.	
	23/6/18		Capt Moore D.N. RAMC arrived to duty from 92nd Divl Train. As our own motor transport had now arrived the other cars temporarily attached were returned to their units. Wrote ADMS asking if anything had as yet been done with regard to my establishment sand.	
	24/5/18		At Col Young verbally with reference to the forthcoming move of 1/3 L F.A. to relieve this unit. I heard cases were admitted today. Complete change of clothing was given. The ground clothes of the patients being sent to Berthonval Farm for degassing.	
	25/5/18		Co mobilized Lieut Morton was detailed to report to 5th H.L.I. to relieve Capt Mansfield who returned to 1/3 Low Fld Amb. Lt Col Dunning RN was evacuated sick today.	WarB

Army Form C. 2118.

2nd L.F. AMBULANCE
R.A.M. CORPS (T).

WAR DIARY
or
INTELLIGENCE-SUMMARY.
(Erase heading not required.)

Instructions regarding War Diaries and Intelligence Summaries are contained in F.S. Regs., Part II. and the Staff Manual respectively. Title pages will be prepared in manuscript.

Place	Date	Hour	Summary of Events and Information	Remarks and references to Appendices
ST. ELOI	25/5/18		In accordance with RAMC Operation Order No 3 this unit on being relieved by 3rd Low Field Ambce took over the A.D.S. at A8 c 8.8. & M.D.Stn at St Eloi (F.8.0.9.4.) vacated by that unit.	War 3
	26/5/18		Capt Lottle Wm was detailed as MO to 1/4 H.L.I. Capt Laird reported at Hdqrs here to proceed (via Army RAMC School of Instruction at No 1 Cavalry Clearing Stn Etne	War 3
	27/5/18		About 0400 this morning the enemy commenced to shell ST ELOI the first shell landed in one of the huts occupied by the personnel of this unit. Causing severe casualties as detailed under.

Killed instantaneously - 10. O.R.
Severely wounded - 6. O.R. Died of Wounds - 5. O.R.
 Slightly wounded - 10. O.R.
Intermittant shelling continued all day but no further damage resulted.
In view of the fact that we are extremely short of MOs with this unit I was unable to proceed to CH. de la Haye to meet 20 to 9am field Ambces for instructional purposes. Only 4 MOs are at present doing duty with this unit, including myself. | War 3 |

Army Form C. 2118.

2nd L.F. AMBULANCE
R.A.M. CORPS (T.)

WAR DIARY
or
INTELLIGENCE SUMMARY
(Erase heading not required.)

Place	Date	Hour	Summary of Events and Information	Remarks and references to Appendices
ST ELOI	28/5/18		Capt. Land & 1 Sergeant left to proceed to R.A.M.C. School of Instruction Blois.	WarB
	28/5/18		1 NCO & 30 OR reinforcements R.A.M.C. reported from 9th Bde. R.F.A. As instructed 32 O.R. left to report to O.C. 410th Field Company R.E. Aux Rietz at 10 am to take down 4 huts at the A.D.S.	WarB
	29/5/18		3. O.R - R.A.M.C. reinforcements reported from R.F.A.	WarB
	30/5/18		As instructed Capt. Moore P.W. was detailed to proceed to U.K. with instructions to report at the War Office on expiry of his present contract. 1st June 1918. Capt. McKenzie W.L. reported for duty from 1/1st Low. Fld. Amb. He was despatched to the A.D.S. to take charge of that station. Accompanied by an R.E. Officer I went over the site for the new M.D.S. at ST ELOI (F.9.c.9.5.) pointed out to him the sites which the ADMS had suggested for the huts. He commences erecting the huts tomorrow & intends sinking them about 2 feet for additional safety.	WarB

Army Form C. 2118.

2nd L. F. AMBULANCE
R. A. M. CORPS (T).

WAR DIARY
or
INTELLIGENCE SUMMARY.

(Erase heading not required.)

Instructions regarding War Diaries and Intelligence Summaries are contained in F. S. Regs., Part II. and the Staff Manual respectively. Title pages will be prepared in manuscript.

Place	Date	Hour	Summary of Events and Information	Remarks and references to Appendices
ST ELOI	31/5/18		During the month 20 Off. 487 O.R. were admitted to this Amblce of whom 8 Off. 136 O.R. were wounded. 4 1 Off. 11 O.R. gassed cases. On 26th inst I wrote ADMS requesting an interview with the DDMS XVIII Corps with regard to an adverse report which the ADMS had put in regarding my application for a Command. On 29th and a reply was received stating that at present the DDMS XVIII Corps is away & the ADMS is acting for him. I then requested an interview with the DMS 1st Army in the absence of DDMS XVIII Corps. On the 30th May I again wrote ADMS re my request for an interview with the DMS. No replies have as yet been received by me regarding these requests	WaB

WaBurn Major
2nd L. F. AMBULANCE
R. A. M. CORPS (T).

Army Form C. 2118.

2nd L. F. AMBULANCE
R.A.M. CORPS (T).

WAR DIARY
or
INTELLIGENCE SUMMARY.
(Erase heading not required.)

Instructions regarding War Diaries and Intelligence Summaries are contained in F. S. Regs., Part II. and the Staff Manual respectively. Title pages will be prepared in manuscript.

Place	Date	Hour	Summary of Events and Information	Remarks and references to Appendices
			APPENDIX I	
			Arrangements for evacuation from Main Battle Stations by Canal area	SC 9 & 9¼ Ref Map France Sheet 36A 1/40000
			The Canal de la Lys divides the evacuating area into two equal parts and would require to be worked independently as there is no bridge between the point J27c in advance of our line and the bridge at Ferry J28d. R. dublin. I propose to have a Dressing Station near the cross roads at J31c where no buildings available all being occupied. Near here I propose to erect a stell proof "Elephant". The cases would be evacuated by motor car to the M.D.S. situated at our present Hdqrs where the huts would provide good accommodation for patients. The L doctor would evacuate also by Motor car from Farm Lowe Dressing Station situated at J 30 @ 8.4. The roads are good available for Motor Ambulance Wagons. A serviceable road leads from main road to A.D.S. The bearers would in both sectors form a chain from R.A. Posts and funcunable tyred stretcher carriers could be used to convey patients from R.A. Posts to A.D. Station. The evacuations from M.D.S. would be via Rly. Crossing at Drew- bridge J 32. 8. 3	

Army Form C. 2118.

2nd L. F. AMBULANCE
R. A. M. CORPS (T).

WAR DIARY
or
INTELLIGENCE SUMMARY.
(Erase heading not required.)

Place	Date	Hour	Summary of Events and Information	Remarks and references to Appendices
APPENDIX I			I propose to have no collecting station but to evacuate from A.D.S. direct to M.D.S. I consider that one section plus the bearers of another section would be required to do the work to my satisfaction and that 2 M.Os should be at each Dressing Station.	

Appendix II

Arrangements for evacuation of patients from 151st Bde area.   Ref Map Maroeuil 1/20000

CHAUDIERE bearers are evacuated from R.A.P. at top of HAYTER trench (T.8.c.9.5) by Ambulance bearers along Hayter trench to Relay Post situated under Rly Embankment at T.13.d.4.8. from Relay Post cases are carried down White trail (Duck Board over open) to A.D.S.

Cases from Support R.A.P. (Railway Embankment T.13.b.5.3) are carried direct to A.D.S. via White trail by Ambce bearers.

The two R.A.Ps and the Relay Post have each 4 bearers at present. One Sergeant is in immediate charge of these bearers.

at A.D.S. chandiere 2 Off. 280 R.

VIMY left R.A.P. (T.16.c.4.9.) to A.D.S. during day by bearers down trail and Canada trenches to Relay Post at T.20.B.3.6.

Army Form C. 2118.

WAR DIARY
or
INTELLIGENCE SUMMARY.
(Erase heading not required.)

2nd L. F. AMBULANCE
R.A.M. CORPS (T).

Place	Date	Hour	Summary of Events and Information	Remarks and references to Appendices
		APPENDIX I contd.	Thence by Light Rly tram to A.D.S. During night by Light Rly tram from R.A.P. to A.D.S. from R.A.P. at T.29.a.4.1. by bearers to Relay Post at T.26.d.8.9. via Hudson & C.P.R. trenches and Meray Alley. From Relay Post cases are carried by bearers to cutting on Rly Embankment (T.26.c.8.9.) from where they are evacuated by trolley to A.D.S. Under favourable circumstances the bearers can work over the open from R.A.P. at T.29.a.4.1. to Relay Post. From Support R.A.P. at B.9.c.9.1. cases are evacuated direct to A.D.S. by light railway. At each R.A.P. – 4 bearers at Relay Post on night line of evacuation – 8 bearers at Relay Post on left line of evacuation – 4 bearers Sergeant in charge of Rt. line Corporal in charge of left line. At A.D.S. 2 Officers 10. O.R. I.O.R. employed as runners. From A.D.S. patients are evacuated to M.D.S. by Motor Amber. The late occupants of Two sector evacuated to a C.C.S. direct from Chandere d'Nurry by Light Rly Train. This tram normally	

Army Form C. 2118.

2nd L. F. AMBULANCE
R.A.M. CORPS (T.)

WAR DIARY
or
INTELLIGENCE SUMMARY.
(Erase heading not required.)

Place	Date	Hour	Summary of Events and Information	Remarks and references to Appendices
Appendix II cont^d			arrived at Chaudière about 0300. The number of patients being phoned to Rly. Authorities from a point about 400 yards from A.D.S. at Chaudière, this was utilised when the A.D.S. became congested and the train did not pass through AUX RIETZ. Artillery Post. (1 N.C.O. & 2 men) A.S. A.M.O. This post serves a group of heavy batteries all within 100 yards of road. Motor Ambulances can go to part of the main road nearest battery. APPENDIX III A D M S. W E P D. Ref your S.R. 50 of 19th inst. The O.C. Rly cannot run a tram in connection with this post and my stages. The evacuation via VIMEY is impracticable on account of the exposed area over which the bearers would have to traverse also, on account of the greatly increased distance. The evacuation would have to be via TIRED ALLEY, THELUS road to Relay post near Canadian mound, where I have a post already established. The evacuation will be estimated, the evacuation will require to be done by hand or wheel stretcher carriages	

Army Form C. 2118.

WAR DIARY
or
INTELLIGENCE SUMMARY.
(Erase heading not required.)

2nd L.F. AMBULANCE
R.A.M. CORPS (T).

Place	Date	Hour	Summary of Events and Information	Remarks and references to Appendices
AUX RIETZ			APPENDIX IV Arrangements for evacuation by Light Railway	

(A) To Control Officer Aux Riety

I have received the following instructions from ADMS 52 Divn and would be glad if you will give me particulars of arrangements that can be made.

1. Please arrange with Light Railway Control to run a train each evening to collect cases from the Adv. Dressing Stations and bring them to you at D.R.S.

2) Arrangements should be made for a series of trains in the event of heavy casualties.

Arrangements in both cases, giving times and route to be reported to this office.

B) From Control Officer.
Is attached.

I can the arrangements but we must be advised each night if there are cases to be brought out.
As there is scarcely wounded not do for us to run trains eye to the ADS where nothing there for them.

If in the event of heavy casualties we can run a series of trains but we cannot guarantee a regular time for the following reasons

Army Form C. 2118.

2nd L. F. AMBULANCE
R.A.M. CORPS (T.)

WAR DIARY
or
INTELLIGENCE SUMMARY.
(Erase heading not required.)

Instructions regarding War Diaries and Intelligence
Summaries are contained in F. S. Regs., Part II.
and the Staff Manual respectively. Title pages
will be prepared in manuscript.

Place	Date	Hour	Summary of Events and Information	Remarks and references to Appendices
	APP 15 (Contd)		(a) Ammunition has priority. (b) In the event of heavy shelling the track may be broken, which will cause delay while being repaired. (c) As the nights get shorter the running time of the convoy will have to be changed. We cannot go over the ridge in daylight. The route will be direct to Rue Biez via Bas Maisnil and Ivey. Alternate route via Farbus Line Thelus Ivey.	

Army Form C. 2118.

WAR DIARY
or
INTELLIGENCE SUMMARY.
(Erase heading not required.)

Instructions regarding War Diaries and Intelligence Summaries are contained in F. S. Regs., Part II. and the Staff Manual respectively. Title pages will be prepared in manuscript.

17 WO95

1st/3
Vol. 3.
140/3046.

CONFIDENTIAL

WAR DIARY
OF
1/2nd LOWLAND
FIELD
AMBULANCE

From 1/6/18 to 30/6/18.

D. Johnson Scott
Lieut. Col.
O.C. 2nd. Low: Fd. Ambce.
R. A. M. CORPS, T.

COMMITTEE FOR THE
MEDICAL HISTORY OF THE WAR
Date 7 AUG. 1918

Place	Date	Hour	Summary of Events and Information	Remarks and references to Appendices
	June 1918			

WAR DIARY or INTELLIGENCE SUMMARY

Vol 31.

Place	Date	Hour	Summary of Events and Information	Remarks and references to Appendices
Mont St Eloi	1/6/18		Capt Lamb & Sergt Stevenson returned from 1st Army School of Instruction	WarB
	2/6/18		78 O.R. admitted to Hospital today. Uneventful	WarB
	3/6/18		59 O.R. admitted to Hospital today. 25 men & three cook & 98 men of 1/1st L.F.A. in charge of Sgt Gwan were employed at. day in preparing the new Main Dressing Station. I applied at HQrs 156th Bde for personnel to assist in erecting new M.D.Stn but no men were available. Notified O.C. A.D.Stn to detail an M.O. to take sick parade of Bde Transport at Berthonval Farm. 48 O.R. admitted to Hosp today.	WarB
	4/6/18		The enemy shelled the camp this morning. No casualties resulted. Parts of men were employed on M.D.Stn again today. Instructed O.C. A.D.Stn to detail 2 trained gas orderlies to be stationed at the Baths - Neuville St Vaast. The two M.A.C. cars attached to this unit were returned to 8th M.A.C.	WarB

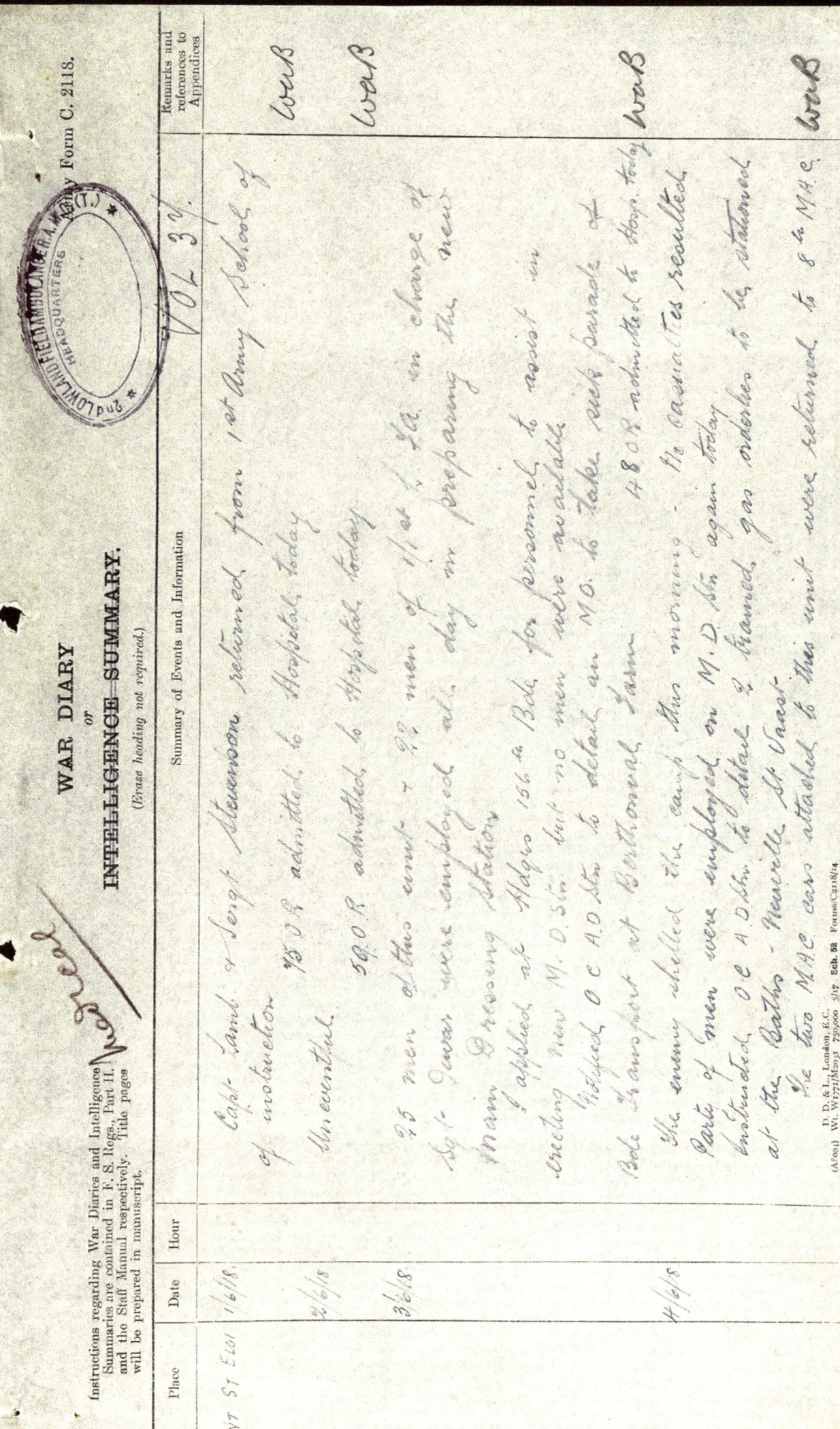

WAR DIARY
or
INTELLIGENCE SUMMARY.
(Erase heading not required.)

Army Form C. 2118.

Place	Date	Hour	Summary of Events and Information	Remarks and references to Appendices
MONT ST ELOI.	4/6/18	Contd	Arrangements were made with O.C. 2ⁿᵈ M.A.C for evacuation of patients to CCS in the future. D.C. 2ⁿᵈ M.A.C. to send Despatch rider daily, who will be informed of the number of cars required.	WaB
	5/6/18		70 O.R. admitted to Hospital today. Capt Black returned from leave to U.K. Party of 7 personnel employed at new M.D. Stn. On 31st ult the body of a man who had been wounded by H.E. shell was brought to this Amb. by an R.A.F car. As no time or identity discs accompanied the body enquiries were immediately instituted to discover the particulars. No their enquiries were undertaken a photographer was sent for to No 1 Mobile X Ray Unit, who arrived the following day. The photos have now been received & sent to ADMS + DAG GHQ. for identification.	WaB
	6/6/18		3 Off. 64 O.R. admitted to Hospital today - mainly P.U.O + Influenza The DDMS XVIII Corps accompanied by ADMS visited camp today Party employed at M.D. Stn. erecting huts. Capt McKenzie returned to 1/1st Lowland Field Ambulance 1 Off. 72 OR admitted to Hospital mainly P.U.O + Influenza	WaB

WAR DIARY
or
INTELLIGENCE SUMMARY.
(Erase heading not required.)

Army Form C. 2118.

Place	Date	Hour	Summary of Events and Information	Remarks and references to Appendices
MONT ST ELOI	7/6/18		Capt. Angus was evacuated sick to Hospital today. ADMS visited and made a careful inspection of the camp.	WaB
	8/6/18		One reinforcement (Cpl L. Hinton) arrived from 56 a Bde R.F.A. 2 O/R + 44 O.R admitted to Hospital today - mainly P.U.O + skin diseases. Party employed at new M.D.S. as usual.	WaB
	9/6/18		2 O/R 64 O.R admitted to Hospital today. Two Medical Officers of the American Medical Corps arrived for duty with this unit. 318100 Pte Stewart Geo. was killed today by the result of the enemy shelling the camp. Party employed at new M.D.Stn as usual.	WaB
	10/6/18		2 O/f, 90 O.R admitted to Hospital - Still mainly P.U.O + skin diseases today. D.D.M.S. XVIII Corps visited the camp today. Lieut Gallacher proceeded to the Colo Dressing Stn for duty. Party employed at new M.D.Stn as usual.	WaB
	16/6/18		56 O.R admitted to Hospital today	WaB

Army Form C. 2118.

WAR DIARY
or
INTELLIGENCE SUMMARY.
(Erase heading not required.)

Instructions regarding War Diaries and Intelligence Summaries are contained in F. S. Regs., Part II. and the Staff Manual respectively. Title pages will be prepared in manuscript.

Place	Date	Hour	Summary of Events and Information	Remarks and references to Appendices
MONT ST ELOI	11/6/18		The personnel of Cols Gregory & Orr were put through Lachrymatory Gas test at LA TARGETTE today. 318494 Cpl Glover J. was detailed for duty at 197th to Bde Hdqrs. 318145 L/Cpl Fleming A. was detailed to report to Director of Roads GHQ with a view to obtaining a commissioned rank in a Quarrying Coy. 6 Offrs 68 O.R. admitted to Hospital today.	WaB
	12/6/18		Capt Goldie rejoined unit from 1/4th H.L.I. 318145 Cpl Strachan were detailed to report at School of Instruction - No 1 COS MAURANS. Capt Black & took over the duties of Capt Black at the Adv Dressing Station. 3Offs 105 O.R. admitted to Hospital today.	WaB
	13/6/18		Capt Lomb left to take over the duties of Capt Black at the Adv Dressing Station 3 Offs 105 O.R. admitted to Hospital today, of whom 49 were Phosgene 36 Trench Stretchers were received & forwarded to O.C. 1/3 L.F.A. for use in the Trenches & to be regarded as French stores. As instructed by ADMS 1 NCO & six men were detailed to report to O.C. 413th Field Coy R.E. at BERTHONVAL FARM baths to assist in the	WaB

WAR DIARY
or
INTELLIGENCE SUMMARY.

Army Form C. 2118.

Place	Date	Hour	Summary of Events and Information	Remarks and references to Appendices
MONT ST ELOI.	13/6/18	Contd	Erection of a disinfector Personnel of unit stationed at MONT ST ELOI. attended gas school today 9 had S.B.Rs tested Party of 1 NCO & 32 men as usual employed in erecting new M.D.S. at F.G.	
	14/6/18		6 Off 95 O.R. admitted to Hospital today. Parties as yesterday employed at new M.D.S. & Bethonval huts Received orders re move of this unit to LES QUATRE VENTS 8 Off 158 O.R. admitted to Hospital today afternoon 119 were P.U.O. cases In accordance with instructions from A.D.M.S. the Holgrs of this unit moved from MONT ST ELOI to site previously occupied by 2/1 North Midland Field Ambce at LES QUATRE VENTS One Motor Car was stationed at MONT ST ELOI for permanent duty for emergency cases.	War B
	15/6/18		For this new emerging ground Bell tents were erected for accomodation of personnel of unit, the huts being reserved for patients 21 Reinforcements arrived for duty with the unit from RAMC Base Depot. 2 Off, 119 O.R. admitted to Hospital today afternoon 59 were P.U.O. cases.	War B War B

WAR DIARY or INTELLIGENCE SUMMARY

Army Form C. 2118.

Place	Date	Hour	Summary of Events and Information	Remarks and references to Appendices
MONT ST ELOI.	16/6/18		Whilst ADMS asking if it is possible to obtain from C.R.E. a sufficient number of posts to enable me to carry on the shelter proof protection of huts. Two huts have been almost completed by the mere previously occupying this site. There is plenty of wire available but no posts to hand. 250 posts are required. Parties employed as usual at Berthonval disinfector & new MDSts. 197 Patients admitted to Hospital today Evacuations 149 our PUO cases. 150 cases were evacuated today.	War3
	17/6/18		ADMS visited & inspected the Camp today. Parties employed as usual on Berthonval disinfector & new MDS-F9. 216 patients admitted to Hospital today Evacuations 198 were PUO Cases.	War3
	18/6/18		DDMS XVIII Corps called today. Arrangements arranged by DDMS - 400 blankets & 50 Stretchers were received today & 200 blankets were handed over to 1/1 at Low Holland	War3

WAR DIARY or INTELLIGENCE SUMMARY

Army Form C. 2118.

143rd LOWLAND FIELD AMBULANCE

Place	Date	Hour	Summary of Events and Information	Remarks and references to Appendices
NEVERS	18/6/18	Contd.	Parties employed as usual at Bethrouvd. Throughout from M.D. Sh. 111 patients admitted to Hospital today of whom 92 were P.U.O. cases	WaR
	19/6/18		Capt. Lester R.A.M.C. was detailed for duty as M.O. i/c R.S. & as instructed by A.D.M.S. T/Sgt Spence was notified to report to O.C. 5 Canadian Sanitary Sec. non 5r 6101 with 30 men for the purpose of thoroughly disinfecting huts for 137 to Bde who are being occupied. 305 patients admitted to hospital of whom 290 were P.U.O. cases. 305 cases were evacuated today. Short of Medical Officers.	WaR
	20/6/18		Employed at Hqtrs here - Lieut. Henderson myself - at A.D.Sh. Major Land & Lieut Gallagher. In accordance with instructions from A.D.M.S. a morning & an evening parade of the personnel of the unit was held during which each man used a permanganate solution as a gargle mouth wash. This was done as a preventative during the epidemic of P.U.O.	WaR

Army Form C. 2118.

WAR DIARY
or
INTELLIGENCE SUMMARY.
(Erase heading not required.)

Place	Date	Hour	Summary of Events and Information	Remarks and references to Appendices
4 VENTS	30/5/18	Cont'd	Instructions were also issued to the personnel as to pay particular attention to the cleanliness of the teeth. This present epidemic of PUO appears to be due to a pneumococcus affecting the mouth, nose & throat. It is characterised by a temperature of between 102° - 104° the first day of attack, with severe throbbing headaches. The patient is generally regains his normal health at the end of about 7 to 8 days, but is generally constipated. Parties employed as usual at Berthonval, Champfête and new M.D.Stn. 218 patients were admitted today, of whom 198 were PUO cases.	WarB
	31/5/18		A.D.M.S. visited with reference to the opening of an auxiliary hospital for the reception of cases of P.U.O. at CHAMBLAIN L'ABBÉ. The accommodation of this hospital is to be 800. & to be staffed by personnel of 20 O. Rank Fld. Amb s, but to be under the supervision of this unit & to be known as a detachment of this unit.	WarB

WAR DIARY
or
INTELLIGENCE SUMMARY.

(Erase heading not required.)

Army Form C. 2118.

1/1st LOWLAND
FIELD
AMBULANCE.

Place	Date	Hour	Summary of Events and Information	Remarks and references to Appendices
4 VENTS	21/6/15	contd	5000 Blankets were received today for use at auxiliary hospital. This hospital was opened at once, & prepared to receive patients. 286 patients were admitted today of whom 2 ## were P.U.O. cases. Parties still employed at Perthonval desinfector & new M.D. Sta.	WaB
	22/6/15		Capt Black & Sergt Strachan returned from R.A.M.C School of Instruction (No 1 CCS) The working party employed at new M.D. Stn. were withdrawn. 1 NCO, 1/Sgt/major & 36 bearers sent to report to OC 1/3rd L.F.A. to be employed as stretcher bearers. 545 patients were admitted today of whom 522 were P.U.O. cases.	WaB
	23/6/15		Two rats were found in a dying condition in one of our huts. As no poison had been put down it appeared strange that they should be found in such a condition. I therefore had one of the bodies wrapped in lint saturated in a solution of formaldehyde, placed in a box & forwarded to OC Field Laboratory for bacteriological examination. Report received later that nothing abnormal was found.	WaB

WAR DIARY
or
INTELLIGENCE SUMMARY.

Army Form C. 2118.

1/2nd ZEALAND FIELD AMBULANCE

Place	Date	Hour	Summary of Events and Information	Remarks and references to Appendices
4 VENTS	23/6/18	Contd	128 patients were admitted, of whom 114 were P.U.O. cases	WeB
	24/6/18		Capt D Jobson M.O. M.C. arrived and took over the command of the unit. A thorough inspection of the Hospital grounds & Hutments was made, & indents submitted for necessaries to replenish & improve the appearance of the Hospital, which was found to be in an unsatisfactory condition. 97 patients were admitted of whom 79 were P.U.O cases	FB.
	25/6/18		I instructed that C.Os parade would be held at 0900 each morning, during which I inspect the personnel of the unit. At 1000 each morning I make a thorough inspection of the Hospital, & the grounds & watch the progress of the work of the personnel, who are now mainly employed in repairing & improving the condition of the Hospital.	FB.

Army Form C. 2118.

WAR DIARY
or
INTELLIGENCE SUMMARY.
(Erase heading not required.)

Place	Date	Hour	Summary of Events and Information	Remarks and references to Appendices
4 VENTS.	23/6/18		100 patients were admitted today 41 of whom were PUO cases. I visited & inspected the WW. 6d. Post today & made several suggestions for improvements.	₣p
	26/6/18		Capt. Goldie returned from 1/4 R.S.L today. I accompanied Sergt. Black & Corpl. Mullan, who were proceeding to 157th Bde Hqrs to be interviewed by B.q.C. with reference to obtaining commissioned rank in the R.A.F. As instructed by A.D.M.S. Lieut HEMPSTED was detailed for duty with Corps H.Qrs. A marked improvement was found during my inspection of both personnel & hospital today. 92 patients were admitted today 64 of whom were PUO cases. At 0900 - H.A.S. wagons arrived from Hal L.H. for the purpose of drawing gravel at FOSSE 9 on the authority of D.A.D.R. The 157th Bde held sports at ST. ELOI today	₣v
	27/6/18		95 patients were admitted to Hospital 68 of whom were PUO cases	₣v

Army Form C. 2118.

WAR DIARY
or
INTELLIGENCE SUMMARY.
(Erase heading not required.)

Place	Date	Hour	Summary of Events and Information	Remarks and references to Appendices
4 VENTS.	28/6/18		I visited the W.W.C.P. at Aux Riets. During my inspection of the Hospital, Huts etc still further improvements were noticed. Time & trouble for which nothing have now been obtained, with which not improvements are being made to the inside of the Huts etc. Wrote A.D.M.S. asking for a definite ruling as to the questions of seniority of Captains Lamb & Black. The matter was referred to Corps H.Q. who ruled that Capt Lamb is the senior. I instructed Capt Lamb to visit the W.W.C.P. of 20th & 24th Div with A/Sgt Black to pick up any tips possible. 101 patients were admitted to Hospital today, of whom 82 were Q.U.O.	D
	29/6/18		Submitted to A.D.M.S. sketch of a St John's Ambulance stretcher made short to fit special ambulance cars which I saw recently on a London Station platform. This was with reference to an inquiry by D.G. a few weeks ago about whether shortened stretchers could be used in forward areas	D

Army Form C. 2118.

WAR DIARY
or
INTELLIGENCE SUMMARY.
(Erase heading not required.)

Instructions regarding War Diaries and Intelligence Summaries are contained in F. S. Regs., Part II. and the Staff Manual respectively. Title pages will be prepared in manuscript.

[2/1 LOWLAND FIELD AMBULANCE]

Place	Date	Hour	Summary of Events and Information	Remarks and references to Appendices
4 VENTS.	29/6/18	cont.	A suggestion for a Divisional Ambulance Badge was submitted to me by Capt. Black. I agreed with him that it was an admirable distinguishing badge for the purpose, and on obtaining the approval of the other O.C. Ambces of the Division I submitted the design to A.D.M.S. for consent to be given to wear same. Copy of design is shown in margin. Field Ambulances will be distinguished by the Colour of the L. 1st Low Hland -3/4 Colour Red. 2nd Low -1/2 Colour Yellow. 3rd Low 3/4 Colour Blue. 62 patients were admitted today of whom 46 were D&O cases.	⚑ ⚑
	30/6/18		Submitted to A.D.M.S. A.F. W 3342 re. absorbment of Capt Lamb to Major, also claims for acting rank as Lieut Colonel on behalf of Major Burns for period 2/5 - 23/5/8. As the result of about an hour & a half's "nail hunt" today no less than between 30 & 40 lbs of nails have been collected. 2 H.O. Horses were received today. 42 patients were admitted to Hospital today of whom 21 were D&O.	

P. Tolson Test
Lieut. Col.
O.C. 2nd. Low. Fd. Amb.
R.A.M. CORPS T.

WAR DIARY
or
INTELLIGENCE SUMMARY.
(Erase heading not required.)

Army Form C. 2118.

1/2 Lowland Fd Amb

Vol 4

140/3/3/2

Confidential
War Diary
of
2nd Lowland Fd Ambulance R.A.M.C. (T.)
HEADQUARTERS

July 1918.

COMMITTEE FOR THE
MEDICAL HISTORY OF THE WAR
Date 6 SEP. 1918

D Dobson Scott
Lieut. Col.
O.C. 2nd. Low. Fd. Amb.
R.A.M. CORPS. T.

Place	Date	Hour	Summary of Events and Information	Remarks and references to Appendices
	July 1918			

WAR DIARY
or
INTELLIGENCE SUMMARY.
(Erase heading not required.)

Army Form C. 2118.

Place	Date Hour	Summary of Events and Information	Remarks and references to Appendices
LES QUATRE VENT W.9 central sheet 44 B.	June 1918. 1st	Detachment at CAMBLAIN L'ABBE treating P.U.O (Pyrexia uncertain origin; an influenza like epidemic) closed down today.	S/A.
	2nd	M.T.C.P. moved from A.8.c.8.8. sheet 44 B at AUX RIETZ to site of M.D.S. at A.8.c.5.5. sheet at AUX RIETZ on the move of the latter to ST ELOY.	S/A.
	3rd	Capt. BLACK to 1/4th R.S.F. for temporary duty during absence on leave of M.O. to thereof.	S/A.
	4th	All available personnel are employed continuously on improving the dilapidated premises of hospl. & gas masks worn by all personnel for 3/hour in morning as test. All horses harnessed up from a state of readiness in 7 to 12 minutes.	S/A.
	5th	Improvements continue to be carried out at HBrs. L'Raine. Personnel. Hutting &c. being arranged by R.E. at old M.D.S.	S/A.

Instructions regarding War Diaries and Intelligence Summaries are contained in F. S. Regs., Part II. and the Staff Manual respectively. Title pages will be prepared in manuscript.

WAR DIARY
or
INTELLIGENCE SUMMARY.
(Erase heading not required.)

Army Form C. 2118.

Place	Date	Hour	Summary of Events and Information	Remarks and references to Appendices

to make it suitable as a W.W.C.P. the arrangement made being as below.

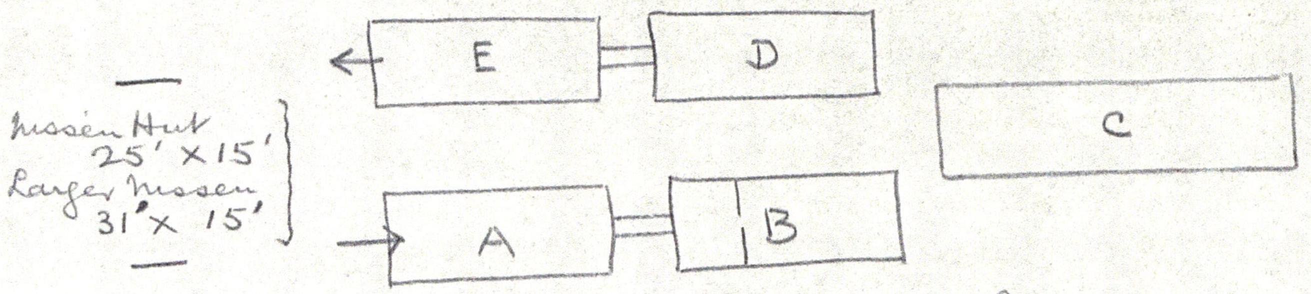

Patients enter ordinary sized Nissen Hut A, a Waiting Room with Buffet and proceed to
B which has 1st a recording room } thence to
2nd an A.T.S. room }
C a Nissen hut (nearly double length) which is Dressing Room: thence to
D + E Evacuation Rooms (one of which will be sure to have some lying cases) with Buffet.

D. D. & L., London, E.C. (A5004) Wt. W1771/M2031 750,000 5/17 Sch. 52 Forms/C2118/14

5/P

WAR DIARY
INTELLIGENCE SUMMARY

Army Form C. 2118.

Place	Date Hour	Summary of Events and Information	Remarks and references to Appendices
	July 1/18	If there is shelling in that neighbourhood, AUX RIETZ (A 8 c central sheet 44 B) all patients will have to be treated in caves or dug outs near by under more or less hastily improvised but now organised arrangements the cave or dug outs depending on the exact location of the shelling.	
BES 4 VENTS	6ᵗʰ	Sick admitted during week ending Sat. 6ᵗʰ inst. 209 b.c.e.s. ══ 118 * DHs Transferred to D.R.S. 54 Returned to duty 3 Remaining 6/7/18 37 * mainly P.U.O. cases sent down under orders during first 3 days of this period.	

WAR DIARY or INTELLIGENCE SUMMARY

Army Form C. 2118.

Place	Date	Hour	Summary of Events and Information	Remarks and references to Appendices
LES 4 VENTS	July 7/18		Inspected Batts. at NEUVILLE ST. VAAST under new training. Them are in the event of a large minen[w]erfer – gas casualties occurring in the Dut. Minor alterations were suggested to R.E. to carry out so that cases would be dealt with as in attached sketch. (vide next page).	S/D
"	8th		O/Smd. inspected Headquarters Field Amb'ce.	S/D
"	9th		Work of improving Fields Amb'ce site is being continued.	S/D
"	10th		Complete subdivision of Field Amb'ce personnel into sections has been carried out in order to improve organisation. Care of equipment & working together in the unit. By 6 p.m. 12th will be staffed by C sections, and information of a few bearers from C. section only	S/D

WAR DIARY
or
INTELLIGENCE SUMMARY.

Army Form C. 2118.

Place	Date	Summary of Events and Information	Remarks and references to Appendices
LES 4 VENTS	July 11th/18	Routine Day – Thundery weather – improvement in state of hutting continues.	S/O
"	12th	P.U.O. Epidemic slim. ceased & numbers of sick decreased considerably.	S/O
	13th	Sick admitted during week ending 13th = 100 Evacuated to C.C.S.s 48 Transferred to D.T.Rs 8 Returned to duty 11 Remaining 13/7/18 69	S/O
	14th	Arrangements made with O/C 73 Amb. re site at ESTRÉE CAUCHIE to take it over and open it as VIII Corps Skin Centre.	S/O
	15th	Weather very wet & showery, though warm. Weather warm & no rain during day but violent thunderstorm in night. Enemy Offensive near Rheims reported but situation quiet on British front.	S/O

Army Form C. 2118.

WAR DIARY or INTELLIGENCE SUMMARY.

(Erase heading not required.)

Summary of Events and Information

SCHEME OF ARRANGEMENT OF 32ⁿᵈ DIVˡ GAS CENTRE AT BATH HOUSE

N.B. Medical Officer to hold a class of instruction at least once a week at the Bath House.

```
                    ┌──────────────┬──────────────┐
                    │OFFICERS' BATH│ ENGINE ROOM  │
                    │1 R.A.M.C.    │              │
                    │orderly       │ 2 Engineers  │
                    │(Non Med.     │              │
                    │ orderly)     │              │
                    ├──────────────┴──────────────┤
                    │          SPRAYS             │
                    │   o   o   o   o   o         │
                    │      1 Non Medical Orderly  │
                    ├──────────────┬──────────────┤
                    │ Hot Soda     │  STORE ROOM  │
                    │ Baths to be  │ for clothing │
                    │ used as dip  │ special gas  │
                    │              │ centre stores│
                    │ NOT TO BE    │ lists of     │
                    │   USED       │ which are to │
                    │              │ be inventoried│
                    │              │ Clean clothing│
                    │              │ weekly & copy │
                    │              │ sent to H.Q.  │
                    │              │ issued        │
                    │              │ Non Med Orderly│
                    │              │ also for patients│
                    │              │ awaiting evacuation│
                    ├──────────────┼──────────────┤
                    │ UNDRESSING   │ DRESSING ROOM│
                    │    ROOM      │(1 R.A.M.C.   │
                    │(1 R.A.M.C.   │ orderly)     │
                    │ orderly      │(2 Non med.   │
                    │ 1 Non Med.   │  orderlies)  │
                    │ orderly)     │              │
                    │              │     N.B.     │
                    │Orderlies to  │R.A.M.C. Sgt  │
                    │wear box      │and Non Med.  │
                    │respirator,   │Glac to take  │
                    │gloves &      │move from one │
                    │antiseptic    │room to another│
                    │bandages for  │directing and │
                    │patients      │organising    │
                    │belonging, and│traffic       │
                    │to help       │              │
                    │patients in   │              │
                    │every way.    │              │
                    │Patients to   │              │
                    │undress and   │              │
                    │rapidly       │              │
                    │through the   │              │
                    │clothing into │              │
                    │coverall      │              │
                    │windows into  │              │
                    │veranda but to│              │
                    │be replaced and│             │
                    │sent in sacks │              │
                    └──────────────┼──────────────┤
                                   │ TREATMENT    │MEDICAL OFFICER'S
                                   │   ROOM       │INSPECTION
                                   │              │   ROOM
                                   │3 R.A.M.C.    │1 R.A.M.C.
                                   │orderlies     │orderly
                                   └──────────────┴──────────────┘
```

(3 Non Medical Orderlies)

X **VERANDAH FOR SORTING GASSED CLOTHING**
Orderlies to sort out clothing, service dress, shirts, socks, boots, equipment &c all clothing to be aired, packed in sacks and sent to Divisional Form Throat disinfection Boots to be in another box and will be stored of lime returned to patient Rifles & arms to be washed in Soda Sol. dried and returned to patient

↑ DIRECTION OF TRAFFIC

Police guard to be erected on railed up only when gas centre is opened

⊕ DIVISIONAL GAS CENTRE

Remarks and references to Appendices

Offr I.

Procedure to be adopted in M.Os inspection Room

No recording to be attempted but one of the printed cards (S) (3)(C) or (D) will be given to each patient a note of treatment if any required being added there to and the patient sent on to W.W.C.P. for according area of disposal

The railing to be erected Evacuation to W.W.C.P. by horsed ambulance wagons or cars

5p.

WAR DIARY or **INTELLIGENCE SUMMARY**
Army Form C. 2118.

Place	Date	Summary of Events and Information	Remarks and references to Appendices
LES 4 VENTS	July/1/18		
	16"	Took over unit Tent subsidy B section under Lt GALLACHER of C section (from WWCP temporarily) Site of Field Amb. & a VIII Corps Skin Centre at ESTREE CAUCHIE. Tentsubsidy A section & under Major BURNS of B section is at HDrs. with accommodation for 100 cases. C Section tentsubsidy Major LATTS is at WWCP at AUX RIETZ still & staff Gas Centre too in emergency. Bearers doing improvements etc. are distributed among the Three places: vide Role of D. Aub's *	Apps II s/p
	17"	VIII Corps Gas Centre opened this afternoon. (Scheme of arrangements attached) (*	App III s/p
	18"	Improvements almost completed on second Hospital Hutch HDrs. Weather very changeable & Thunderstorms frequent.	s/p

WAR DIARY
or
INTELLIGENCE SUMMARY.

(Erase heading not required.)

Army Form C. 2118.

Place	Date	Summary of Events and Information	Remarks and references to Appendices
LES 4 VENTS	July 19th	All patients evacuated to I.C.C.S. (which nearer Convalescent Patients mainly & this acts as a Rest Station) today in preparation for move tomorrow.	D/p
" " "	20th	Transport left by road at 9.30 a.m. & reaching for about 2 hours en route arrived at AUCHEL (HAZEBROUCK 5A. F.6) about 4 p.m. Personnel marched to St ELOI station arriving as ordered at 2 p.m. Train left at 8.10 p.m. & after much delay en route arrived at CALONNE - RICAURT station at 2.10 a.m. on	D/p
" " "	21st	21st inst. arriving by road at AUCHEL about 3.10 a.m. Weather changeable & thunderstorms frequent. Troops wire up at Hotel de Ville.	D/p

WAR DIARY
or
INTELLIGENCE SUMMARY.

Army Form C. 2118.

Place	Date	Hour	Summary of Events and Information	Remarks and references to Appendices
AUCHEL			Sick admitted dur: week ending 20"inst: 120 Discharges to Duty 45 Evacuated to CCS 64 Transferred to DRS. 80	S/p
	22.		Field Amb:ce opened up at AUCHEL is now organized to receive up to 70 patients, including up to 12 cases of scabies. Improvements started at once in hospital accommodation, cookhouse, men's billets etc.	S/p
"	23.		Bye. sick (157th Infy. Bge.) are collected as below @ numbers requiring collection are notified by Bge. at 10 a.m. & horse ambulance does a round the morning.	S/p

WAR DIARY
INTELLIGENCE SUMMARY.

Army Form C. 2118.

Place	Date	Summary of Events and Information	Remarks and references to Appendices
	July 1/18	D.A.C. & R.A. sick are collected by motor amb: car which then calls at PERNES for sick of Div. H.Q. & details in PERNES each morning. Each afternoon if required an ordinary amb: is done at 3 pm to Regs. at PERNES. Urgent cases civilian (a large clinic is seen at 10 am. daily) military and collected & evacuated as required during the day & night. It is estimated that 1 horse amb & 1 car & 1 motor amb & car should be able to do all ordinary collections & evacuations for the Bge. area incl. R.A. & D.A.C. units.	F/P
AUCHEL	24th	Numbers of sick are small. Thunderstorms on Friday. In addition to considerable improvements to Hospital wards	F/P

WAR DIARY
or
INTELLIGENCE SUMMARY.
(Erase heading not required.)

Army Form C. 2118.

Place	Date	Hour	Summary of Events and Information	Remarks and references to Appendices
AUCHEL	25th		in Hotel de Ville. Unit is training in squads of physical drill, hammerstone being completed, overhauled, outside & inside repaired, points etc. + lectures on Thomas's splint, gas defence etc. are taking place.	S/p
"	26th		Frequent thunderstorms. Numbers of sick are small. S/p	
			18 scabies are being treated in three stages as below.	

	Tub bath	Sulphur ointment	Clean clothing	Stage
1st day m.		—	—	
e.	—			
2nd day m.	—			
e.		—		
3rd day m.		—		→ I
e.	—			
4th day m.	—			
e.		—		→ II
5th day m.	—			
e.		—		
6th day m.			—	→ III → for discharge to duty or transfer to a dermatic case.

S/p

WAR DIARY or INTELLIGENCE SUMMARY

Army Form C. 2118.

Place	Date	Hour	Summary of Events and Information	Remarks and references to Appendices
AUCHEL			Each patient on admission is given a card on above string. Each part of the treatment is given is crossed off; thus — , ⊥ , + . The cases so far are mild + can be cured within the six days both of the presence of weari of the septic serum complications secondary thereto.	
	27th		Number of Patients admitted for week ending 27th: 771 discharged to duty 4 Evacuated to C.C.S. 33	S/D
"	28th		Weather thundery.	S/D
"	29th		Orders for move to XVIII Corps in which 52nd Divn is at present, to take over Arras front from Canadian Corps came in about noon (September number). All patients, not "cures" today, were evacuated to XIII Corps Main Centre by	S/D

WAR DIARY
or
INTELLIGENCE SUMMARY.
(Erase heading not required.)

Army Form C. 2118.

Place	Date	Hour	Summary of Events and Information	Remarks and references to Appendices
AUCHEL	July 1/18		Arrangement check with Bdsns. XIII Corp. All others sick were, unless fit for duty sent to C.C.S. (31 in number); all informations were shared of cleaning, renovating equipment, clothes, uniforms packed as far as possible.	S/A
AUCHEL	30th July		Marched with 157th Infy. Bge. to BARLIN. Weather very hot, close & sultry.	S/A
BARLIN	31st "		Marched into Bge. H MAROEUIL taking over field Ambe site L.4.a.60.65 (sheet 44 B.N.W.) as Divnl. M.D.S. Advance parties were sent on by empty motor ambd cars & by 6 pm. A.D.S. at ECURIE & all forward posts had been taken over from 11th Canadian Field Ambe (for details vide next month). D. Johnson Col. Col. O.C. 1/2 Durl. 2o Amb =	S/A

To O/c W.W.C.P	To O/c W.W.C.P.	To O/c W.W.C.P	To O/c W.W.C.P
M.D.S. by Car	D.R.S by Wagon	M.D.S by Car	D.R.S by Wagon

Appx B I.

To O/c W.W.C.P	To O/c W.W.C.P	To O/c W.W.C.P.	To O/c W.W.C.P
C.C.S. by Lt Rly	Return to Duty	C.C.S by Lt Rly	Return to Duty

Amended Bath and Treatment Summary.

Date		Tub	Spray	Sulphur Ointment	Clean Clothing	Name of Ward	Stage of Case
1st	M	—	—	—	—	—	—
	E	1	1	1	1	A	1
2nd	M	—	1	1	—	A	1
	E	—	1	—	—	A	1
3rd	M	—	1	—	—	A	1
	E	—	1	—	—	A	1
4th	M	1	1	1	1	B	2
	E	—	1	1	—	B	2
5th	M	—	1	—	—	B	2
	E	—	1	—	—	B	2
6th	M	1	1	1	1	C	3
	E	—	1	1	—	C	3
7th	M	—	1	—	—	D or Discharge	4 or Discharge
	E	—	—	—	—		
8th	M						
	E						

Routine to be adopted in (VIII) Corps Skin Centre for Scabies.

(1) All paptients will arrive between 2 & 3 p.m.

(2) Divisions will usually send cases as transfers to 1/2nd. Low. Fd. Ambce. (VIII) Corps Skin Centre)

(3) Corps Troops may arrive as transfers or as direct admissions.

(4) Returns asked for in D.D.M.S. circular will be called for by the cyclist from Hqrs. at 8 a.m. & 3 p.m. daily.

(5) A.F.W3210 will be made out in triplicate for each patient in the reception room.

~~(6)~~ (a) One copy of this will be called for daily by motor cyclist from Hqrs. at 4 p.m. for entering into A.& D. Book at Hqrs.

~~(7)~~ (b) The other will be given to the patient in A.F.W3118a (Field Medical Cards Envelope) and will have on the back thereof a bath and treatment table as attached. Patients will carry this A.F. and envelope with him always even while going through the bath house. On entering the packstore he will show it and have his packstore number entered thereon. On entering the M.I.R. he will show it and be told by the orderly in charge or by the M.O. what processes he has to go through. Before leaving the dressing room the orderly in charge will tick off the processes he has gone through on that tour of the Bath House.

(6) Patients will proceed from reception room to the packstore delivering up their kits for numbering and ~~disfection~~ disinfection, then their Field Medical Card Envelopes and have their packstore number written thereon.

(7) They will proceed to the Bath House passing through in series.
(1) Undressing Room
(2) Medical Inspection Room
(3) Tub Room
(4) Spray Room
(5) Ointment Room
(6) Dressing Room

(8) In undressing Room   All underclothing will be placed in receptacle allotted - outer clothing will be numbered with packstore number, packed in sandbag and given up to be sent to disinfector for treatment and return to packstore. All underclothing similarily before dispatch to laundry will be disinfected.

(9) In M.I.R. A.F.W3210 will be shown and direction given the patient re bath etc. required.

(10) In tub room water will be as hot as passible and patients will scrub each other with a nail brush (one for each patient and boiled after being used each time) Tub bath must last 15 mins.

(11) In Spray Room patient will spend 5 mins., water to be as hot as possible.

(12) After rubbing well with a hard towel patient will be anointed all over thoroughly in the Ointment Room.

(13) In the dressing room pyjamas will be issued and a record will be made on A.F.W3210 of treatment received and patient will proceed to Ward A. and become Stage 1 cases.

(14) Next morning and afternoon (i.e. 2nd. day) all class 1 cases will be passed through the Bath House omitting tub and clean clothing.

(15) Next morning (i.e. 3rd. day) all class 1 cases will go throu through all the processes of the bath house and on emerging with clean pyjamas will enter "B" Ward and become stage 2 cases.

(16) Stage 2 cases will pass through Bath House the same afternoon (i.e. 3rd. day) omitting tub and clean clothing.

(17) Next morning all Stage 2 cases will pass through all the processes of the Bath House and on emerging with clean clothing will enter "C" Ward and become stage 3 cases.

(18) In the afternoon of the same day (i.e. 3rd. day) stage 3 cases will pass through Bath House omitting clean clothing.

(19) Next morning (i.e. 4th. day) all stage 3 cases will pass through all the processes of Bath House and on emerging with clean clothing and service dress previously drawn from packstore by patient and delivered to clean clothing room) will either be discharged to duty or cross to "D" hut and become Class 4 cases i.e. cases in which there are no acari but in which there are secondry skin lesions still to treat.

(20) Stage 4 cases will unless contraindicated pass through Bath House omitting tub and clean clothing daily.   Clean clothing will be given at least once a week.

(21) Patients arriving after 3p.m. will be isolated in a bell tent and start treatment next morning thus shortening stage 1 by 12 hours.

(22) Patients found not to be suffering from Scabies will be isolated in another bell tent and returned to the unit which sent them in the following day.

(23) **Amendment**   Amend scheme so that in each stage there are only two sulphur inunctions (i.e. omit one of the three in stage 1 cases) and that after every second inunction of sulphur spray baths alone followed by the application if necessary of a soothing ointment be given for 24 hours.

vide Amended Summary of Baths as attached

D Dobson Scott
Lt Col

Appx II

THE ROLE OF THE 1/2 ND LOW. FD. AMBCE. IN THE MEDICAL ARRANGEMENTS OF THE 52ND DIVISION ARE AS FOLLOWS.

1. **During normal times.**

   A. **Sick of Units in NEUVILLE ST VAAST AREA** will be collected by, admitted to the W.W.C.P. and thence taken on by Field Ambnce. Cars to M.D.S. at Les 4 Vents.

   B. **Some wounded of Units in NEUVILLE ST VAAST AREA**, including gassed cases may be expected to arrive at W.W.C.P. They will be admitted to W.W.C.P. and transferred by Field Ambnce Cars to M.D.S. of 3rd Low Fd. Ambce. at St. ELOI.

II. **In the Event of Active Operations Ensuing.**

   A. **Wounded** walking cases will be collected at W.W.C.P., and after admission and treatment will be sent by Light Ry., under arrangements made by O.C., W.W.C.P. to Detraining Centre at Mingoval. One N.C.O. and one Orderly will accompany each train to MINGOVAL and be responsible for the care and comfort of the patients. They will report to O.C. Detraining Centre who has orders to send them back to the W.W.C.P. by the most expeditious route. Each Patient will have one blanket, and in wet weather, one waterproof sheet, which the O.C. Detraining Centre has orders to return to W.W.C.P. with the N.C.O. and Orderly. NO Stretcher Cases will be evacuated by the train from W.W.C.P. Motor Lorry stationed at W.W.C.P., may be sent to AUBIGNY-LIGNY Group of C.C.Ss. if a trainload of Patients is not expected soon, and this Lorry will call at Mingoval using the AUBIGNY-MINGOVAL road, (Not Savy-MINGOVAL) to MINGOVAL. In this case also, each Patient will have a blanket and an Orderly will accompany the Patients and return with the Blankets. In the event of the Light Ry. Service breaking down, a Lorry Service will be instituted by Corps.

   (2) **Lying Cases.** The Motor Ambce. Cars of Fld. Ambce. will be used to transfer lying cases which happen to arrive or develop at W.W.C.P. to M.D.S., 3rd. L.F.Amb. at ST. ELOI.

   (3) **Slightly Wounded.**, unfit to return to duty, will be transferred by Horsed Ambnce. to 1/1 L.Fld. Amb., D.R.S. at VILLERS AU BOIS. In all cases, A.T.S. will be administered and recorded on Field Medical Cards and A.F.W. 3210.

   B. **Sick** arriving at W.W.C.P. will be admitted and transferred to 3rd L.F.A., M.D.S. at ST. ELOI, except Lightly Sick, who will be transferred by Horsed Ambce. Wagons to 1st Low. Fld. Ambce. at D.R.S., VILLERS AU BOIS.

Sheet...2...

C.. <u>A Divisional Gas Centre.</u> will be opened at Bath House NEUVILLE ST VAAST by detachment from W.W.C.P. of One Officer and 8 Other Ranks, on receipt of Orders from A.D.M.S., and in the event of large numbers of Yellow Cross Gassed Cases occuring, ~~all~~ All cases must be sent to W.W.C.P. and Cases will be dealt with as other wounded are (Vide Para. II A, Sheet One)

D.. <u>Redistribution of Personnel.</u> Two Officers and all bearers will be sent to reinforce Bearers of 3rd L.F.A. at St. ELOI.

E.. <u>Redistribution of Transport.</u> One Motor Ambce. Car will be posted at W.W.C.P. to convey Lying Cases to M.D.S., at ST. ELOI. Remainder will stand fast at LES 4 VENTS in reserve. Horsed Ambce. Wagons will be stationed at W.W.C.P. to convey slightly wounded and lightly sick to D.R.S.

III. <u>Recording under circumstances I and II.</u>

Field Medical Cards and A.F.W. 3210 (both stamped with the Official Stamp of the Unit) will be made out for all cases ~~at Gas Centre or~~ at W.W.C.P. In the case of Patients sent to LES 4 VENTS M.D.S., both the Fld. Medical Cards and A.F.W. 3210 will accompany the Patients., In all other cases including those of Patients transferred to another Field Ambce., or to C.C.S., Field Medical Cards will accompany the patients and A.F.W. 3210 will be sent to the A. & D. Room at LES 4 VENTS at least every four hours. It is pointed out that amount of A.T.S. and disposal of Patient should be noted on A.F.W. 3210.

1v. Vlll Corps Skin Centre will be run by "B" Section Tent Sub-Division.

16 7/18.

D Jobson Scott
Lieut. Col.
O C 2nd. Low: Fd, Ambce.
R. A. M. CORPS T.

Army Form C. 2118.

WAR DIARY
or
INTELLIGENCE SUMMARY.

(Erase heading not required.)

29 Medical

Vol 5

140/3200,

CONFIDENTIAL

WAR DIARY

1/2nd LOWLAND FIELD AMBCE

R.A.M.C. (T)

From 1st Augt 1918 to 31st Augt 1918.

Stetson Scott
Lieut. Col.
O.C. 2nd. Low. Fd. Amb
R.A.M. CORPS. T.

COMMITTEE FOR THE
MEDICAL HISTORY OF THE WAR
Date 5 OCT 1918

WAR DIARY
or
INTELLIGENCE SUMMARY.
(Erase heading not required.)

Army Form C. 2118.

Place	Date	Hour	Summary of Events and Information	Remarks and references to Appendices
MARDEUIL	Aug 1918	1:-	Ground plan (not drawn exact to scale) of hutage, mainly NISSEN huts unless indicated otherwise by overleaf showing proposed plan of arrangement should accn'e of arduous crane, also indicates alterations required in red (eg. opening up new doors &c &c.)	*App x I
			ADS at ECURIE consists of a long tunnelled dugout with five entrances (two are steep + only to be used in emergency) - others are similar to as below. Rough sketch herewith not drawn to scale *	*App x II S/D

WAR DIARY
or
INTELLIGENCE SUMMARY.
(Erase heading not required.)

Army Form C. 2118.

Place	Date	Hour	Summary of Events and Information	Remarks and references to Appendices
			There is fair accommodation, dressing room, cook house &c. above stores too, but the site at a most important cross Roads is a bad one.	* appx III
			Relay posts are as in attached sketch * showing personnel & a cycle relief is to be kept constantly working from A.D.S. to Relay posts (vide also Appx. IV.).	
			Personnel & duties:-	
			A.D.S. & Relay Posts &c.	
			Capt. BLACK, Lt. NUNN leur from 1st Lowl. Fd. Amb. & C section tent subdivn.	
			& Bearers of B & C sections leas 12 who are relyt at M.D.S. in reserve & circulate every 4th day (i.e. on 4th inst. 2.9. These 12 proceed to A.D.S. by 9.30 a.m. horsed amb.s: Another with stores clears A.D.S. at 1.30 p.m.; this 12 are relieved by 12 from A.D.S. soon).	B/P

WAR DIARY
INTELLIGENCE SUMMARY

Army Form C. 2118.

Place	Date Hour	Summary of Events and Information	Remarks and references to Appendices
	Aug/18	M.D.S. Major LAMB + Lieut Culbremin + 12 reserve bearers of B + C Section + A section incl. specialists ar ABn 29. bootmaker, tailor, painter, joiner &c.	S/p
MARŒUIL	2nd	Heavy rain most of day. " - wounded small in number.	S/p
"	3rd	" " " "	S/p
"	4th	Weather changeable.	S/p
"	5th	Additional 36 bearers from 1/1st Lowland 2/2 Amb's attached to this Amb'ce + reliefs modifies in A.D.S. to the posts. Appendix to 157th Inf. Bge. Defence Scheme sent to Bge *	S/p App. IV
"	6th	Lts FARLOW and CAINE of U.S.A. M.O.R.C. reports for duty. This brings total (medical) Officers in the Bge to 9. 7: of these has Capt GOLDIE and Lt. GALLAGHER are at regimental duties temporarily.	S/p

Army Form C. 2118.

WAR DIARY
or
INTELLIGENCE SUMMARY.
(Erase heading not required.)

Place	Date	Hour	Summary of Events and Information	Remarks and references to Appendices
MAROEUIL	Aug 7/18		Lt. NUNN of 1st Lowland Fd. Amb. has been attached temporarily since we went into the line.	S/p
"	7th		Weather changeable - showery.	S/p
"	8th		In addition to ordinary duties of evacuation all Horse & mechanical transport vehicles are now in turn being painted; all equipment is being overhauled where necessary & repainted; horse standings are being remodelled throughout with beaten in chalk & sand stone & mine-earth on top.	S/p
			For week ending 3rd Aug. Sick admissions 111 - Sick evacuations 37. Sick transfers DRS 72. wounded " 33. wounded " 33.	
"	9th		Normal day. - weather warming up again	S/p
"	10th		3 M.Os from 78th Amer. Fd. Amb. for 4 days instruction of the line.	S/p

WAR DIARY
or
INTELLIGENCE SUMMARY.

(Erase heading not required.)

Place	Date	Hour	Summary of Events and Information	Remarks and references to Appendices

MARŒUIL		11th	For week ending 10th July
			
			      Admitted Evacuated
			    Offs ORs Offs ORs
			Sick 6 58+ 4 26
			Wounded — 27* — 24
			   (*1 died) (+ 2 remain)
			
			Normal evacuations.	

"		12th	" weather very close & warm.	
"		13th	Enemy H.E. shell pitched into their messroom after they had left after tea — wounded mess orderly & 1 M.T. Driver. Two cars were hit also 1 M.E.C. car. The M.A.C. car woodriver Off. under its own [power?]. One of F.A. Aulse cars caught fire at once & burnt itself almost out. The second caught fire from the petrol leak & lit first, has still burst & fire was extinguished therein. All other 5 or 6 shells went well over to Rwy &c. 4 Other men were slightly wounded 2 remained on duty. Warning Ordrs and in eve. re DW being relieved soon by SPDn	s/p s/p s/p Transferred to DRS Off ORs 2 30 — 2 s/p

WAR DIARY or INTELLIGENCE SUMMARY

Place	Date	Hour	Summary of Events and Information	Remarks and references to Appendices
MAROEUIL	14th		Situation on front quiet - enemy shelled Rwy. Sta. in Eve. at some hour or other last evening 7 p.m. today - 1st shell burst high in air beyond Rwy. Sta. - others went also well over this camp & Rwy. Sta. too. 	S/D
"	15th		The shell which hit hospl. ate last eve. was apparently a "short" for Station vicinity. Evacuations few in number except 16 Officers & 170 ORs of 5th H.L.I. were gassed (mustard) in early morn. - they think after sunrise when the gas vapour arose from shell holes round trench. - They reached 2nds. betw. 7 & 10 p.m. with severe to moderate conj. inc. hurts (one with burn on thigh). They were not parked or changed till they reached CCSs. about 6 to 8 p.m. 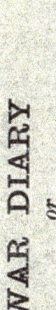	S/D
"	16th		Northern & Southern Bde sectors have been relieved, the former by a Bde of 8th Div. which side slipped.	S/D

WAR DIARY
or
INTELLIGENCE SUMMARY.
(Erase heading not required.)

Army Form C. 2118.

Place	Date	Hour	Summary of Events and Information	Remarks and references to Appendices
MAROEUIL			the latter by a Bge of 51st Divn. Bearer Relay Post were accordingly given up, relief being complete by midnight 15/16th. Cavalry Bge with A.D.S. at ECURIE is to be handed over to a Bge of 8th Divn, relief to be completed by midnight 16/17th.	S/A
	17th		Relief completed by midnight + all details concentrated at H.Q'rs at MAROEUIL — moved off at 6 a.m. 12 kilos to GOUY SERVINS, & billets with small portion of a barn as a detention hosp. (for a few hours) for Bge. sick. Work of improvement of kitchens, detention room, etc. started in afternoon.	S/A
GOUY-SERVINS	18th		Improvements contd.-	S/A
"	19th		" + in addition repainting of last 3 ambulance wagons + last 2 horse transport wagons commenced on. Bge sick are small in numbers + collection by horse amb's in morning is easy, transfers being done in afternoon by one amb. car as a rule.	S/A

WAR DIARY
or
INTELLIGENCE SUMMARY.

Army Form C. 2118.

Place	Date	Hour	Summary of Events and Information	Remarks and references to Appendices
GOUY-SERVINS	Aug. 1918. 20th		Urgent movement order came in in evening & To Aub's moved TD at 11.30pm. until 157th Bge B/group arriving at Y Huttents DUISANS by route march (S1E: G.24.2.7.) at 2.30am on 21st	S/p
DUISANS Sheet 51C (Loc 4 & 6)	21st		Bge group B/effects to move in evening. This evening was postponed late in eve.	S/p
"	22nd		Orders to move came in late in evening.	
BRETENCOURT	23rd		Bge group moved to Bretencourt accompanied it leaving by route march at 1.30am. Took over by 5pm. from 1/3rd N. Mid. Fd. Amb's. Fd. Amb. HQn. in R.15.b. (sheet 51C); also M.D.S. at X Roads in R.29 (sheet 51C) & A.D.S. in M.31.a. (sheet 51B). All Bearers in position by evening & attached Brack Batt's & the remainder out relay posts, under Officers & N.C.O.s.	S/p
FICHEUX	24th		HQn. moved up to concentrate with 1/1Kent Fd. Amb's at M.31.a. (sheet 51B) & later in the day moved on to site between BOISLEUX ST MAUR & BOISLEUX AU MONT at S.11.C.2.9. The Division attacked at	S/p

WAR DIARY
or
INTELLIGENCE SUMMARY.

Army Form C. 2118.

Place	Date	Hour	Summary of Events and Information	Remarks and references to Appendices
			Rain + progress became very rapid. Evacuation thro' an A.D.S. established at S.4.c.9.0 was switched forward later in the day to S.11.a.6.9 & later to BOIRY BECQUERELLE at T.7.b.4.4 and later still to T.1.€.c.9.5 B. Sec. kept subfm This was done by leapfrogging B Sec & vice versa. There was some delay in evacuation as Every into 4 extra cars making a total of 10 the journey back from A.D.S. + BAC DU SUD south of GOUY-EN-ARTOIS on ARRAS—DOULLONS Road was too long. Another factor gave difficult. The bridge over the COJUL river in S.11.c. very soon after completion broke under the weight of a motor lorry & all traffic had to be sent round by another route which had to be patched up in places. Working tirelessly out all night	S/P

WAR DIARY
or
INTELLIGENCE SUMMARY.

Army Form C. 2118.

Place	Date	Hour	Summary of Events and Information	Remarks and references to Appendices
			with Horse ambces cars all post-wen Chaved/wounded by 5 am The weapons to be land. appears to be that OC's ADs Ambcs be push well forward at once Then a rough idea of the battle scheme before they go into the line, that with a rapid advance the Divl cars cannot cope with the increasing distances between ADs & Corps MDS. Corps should have a MAC totally to clear from Divil units & MACs of Army should clear our ADs & CCS.	SP
S11c 29 (Sheet 51B)		25th	A considerable number of cases leaves through from RAPs up to midday almost ADS. dealt with the following patients as attached appx * Appendix V.	Appx V SP

WAR DIARY
or
INTELLIGENCE SUMMARY.
(Erase heading not required.)

Army Form C. 2118.

Place	Date	Hour	Summary of Events and Information	Remarks and references to Appendices
BORY to ECOUVRAL	26th		Moved HQrs forward A.D.S.s moving forward almost daily. to vide Appx VI	Appx VI
In the field	27th		M.D.S. & A.D.S.s moved on Appx VI. A few days. The Div. raced forward over the terrain till captured FONTAINE-LEZ-CROISELLES in its stride & could have reached RIENCOURT but had to first slip the light beyond the SENSÉE river. A.D.S.s were made with light & bearers wagon or Maltese cart impulses from as with ypres (eg river in daylight as far [FONTAINE]) and relay of bearers kept up with fastest point. Horses and wagon were on ap of machine gun fire. Motor ambces + walking wounded G.S. motor lorry pushes forward up the HEWIN Hill to the annual tar road as possible & all cases were cleared early. The only delay being due to M.T. having to go so far back to Corp M.D.S. evacuated it moved forward to BLAIRVILLE	S/P S/P

WAR DIARY
or
INTELLIGENCE SUMMARY.
(Erase heading not required.)

Army Form C. 2118.

Place	Date	Hour	Summary of Events and Information	Remarks and references to Appendices
MERCATEL	Oct/11/18 28th		Ofts, all R.A.P's closed & a much greater strain on was really being taken, mils driven to FONTAINE, but too relieved by 7th Aus. 57 Div moved slowly down to morn & Divisions in MERCATEL	5/11
"	29th		Resting o.c. —	
"	30th		Re-equipping & re-arranging equipment & Sorting out. All wagons are to be equipped to carry 2 gal. lethal tins full of water at once. Must & not[?] [illegible] has not been used in [illegible] very load[?], will be dumped at once, in rest place I our operations Analysis of Routine Casualties in the Aug/s + See App. VII	14/11 VII 15/11

WAR DIARY
or
INTELLIGENCE SUMMARY.

Army Form C. 2118.

Place	Date	Hour	Summary of Events and Information	Remarks and references to Appendices
MERCATEL	Aug. 1918 31st.		Struck camp at 10 a.m. 'B' and 'C' Section sub tent-divisions moved out to T.14.A. at 12 noon, and Capt. Goldie in charge of 'B' and 'C' sections bearer squads went to 157 Brigade Headquarters at 4 p.m. At 9 P.m we relieved the 2.s./Sd. London Field Amb, and took over the A.D.S. at Goirelles. (T23.a.4.6. Sheet 51 b) The system of Medical arrangements was put on a different basis — ~~off the~~ ~~(A)~~ By experience it was found that, in mobile operations conducted over elevated country with bad roads, a Field Ambulance moving with transport, loaded as per Field Service Manual, was unwieldy and could not move quickly enough to keep in touch with the fighting units. To obviate this the following scheme was introduced. (1) "B" & "C" Sections Bearer - Sub divisions were completed from "A"	b/p b/p b/p

WAR DIARY
or
INTELLIGENCE SUMMARY.
(Erase heading not required.)

Army Form C. 2118.

Place	Date	Hour	Summary of Events and Information	Remarks and references to Appendices
			Section Bearers (this was required to replace casualties and of men on leave) and attached under an officer to B.H.Q.	
			2) "A" "B" & "C" sections Tent Sub-Divisions were also completed and instead of moving with the Mob. Table equipment of a complete section went forward with a water cart and a limbered G.S. waggon, which contained the following stores.	
			Medical comfort pannier containing:- Tea 20lb. Sugar...40 lb. Milk...30 tins. Oxo...12 lb. Salt..2 lb. Brandy...2 Botts. Candles..10 lb	
			4" Pannier containing. Bowls..12. Roll of Instruments. Hand Lamps..4 Brushes...30 lb. Stribacen...2. Biobacia store...1 Primus stove..1 Hand towels..12. Castolica tins.. 3 rolls. Lysol...3 tubes. Soap..4 bars Nail Brushes..2. Stomach Warmers..2. 15 Enam. Basins. 1 Haws- Clothing scissors. Enam. feeding cups..2. Zinc Ointment...1. A.T.Syringe...1 A.T.Serum. Safety pins..6 boxes. Adhesive tape...6 rolls. Scissors. 3prs. 2 Surgical Haversacks. 2 Water Bottles 4 Thomas Splints. 1800 3" roller bandages 1500 yds gauze 50 lb cotton wool	S/D

12 Stretchers. 60 blankets. 60 ground sheets. Cook's splinting
4 Camp Kettles. 4 galls Paraffin. 2 galls milk. 2 Dorothy
Hats. 8 gallons water.
2 Cases Biscuits (16 tins)
Operating Lamp.
It will be seen that each tent sub division was fully equipped
to deal with wounded more-fat as to casing and feeding
were concerned.

3) "A" Section Bearer Sub Division had been absorbed in completing "B & C"
Sections, and in addition a Headquarters section was constituted
consisting of O.C., Q.M. Sergt major, Q.M.S, Orderly Room Staff and
store men.
A number of the equipment not required was formed and left
behind in charge of a N.C.O. This could be brought forward as
circumstances arose.

4) The evacuation scheme is as follows:—
"B" section with revised equipment would work A.D.S evacuating
wounded to Advd Field Ambce by means of horsed Ambce Waggons.
"C" section tent sub-division would be held in readiness to move

WAR DIARY
or
INTELLIGENCE SUMMARY.
(Erase heading not required.)

Army Form C. 2118.

Place	Date	Hour	Summary of Events and Information	Remarks and references to Appendices
			forward beyond "B" section when the infantry have advanced, and to form an A.D.S. and keep in touch with the Brigade. Similarly HdQrs would move forward and establish itself in the A.D.S. occupied by "B" section which would then be in readiness for any subsequent forward movement. "A" Section took sub divisions to Heft in reserve ready to move forward to re-inforce "B" or "C" should the necessity arise. Evacuation from A.D.S. to HQ would be carried out by horse Amb. wagons and from HQ to C.M.D.S. by motor ambulance cars, or Should circumstances be favourable horsed waggons would proceed beyond A.D.S. and motor ambulances could circulate direct from A.D.S. to Corps Main Dressing Stn.	D/D

31/8/18.

D. Tobson Capt
Col
OC 1/2 Lowl. Fd Amb

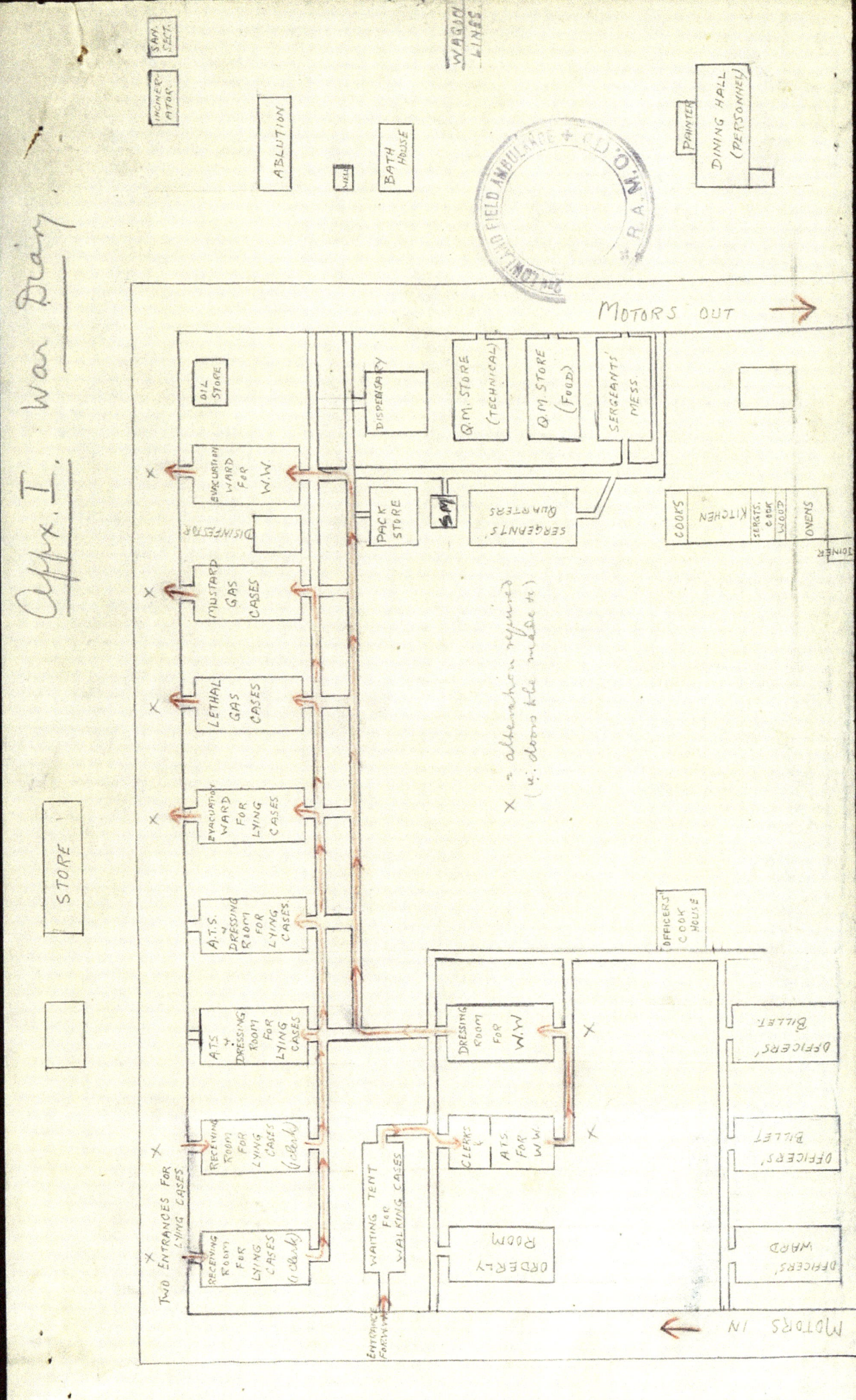

Appx. I. War Diary

Total Battle Casualties on Western Front from 17-4-18 to 28-8-18.

SR 168

	S.M.	QMS	S/Sgt.	Sergt.	Cpls.	L/Cpls	Ptes.	Totals
Killed	-	-	-	-	-	-	12	12
Died of Wounds	-	-	-	-	-	-	4	4
Wounded to C.C.S.	-	-	-	2	2	1	20	25
" Remained at duty	1	-	-	1	-	2	10	14
Totals	1	-	-	3	2	3	46	55

Analysis of above Casualties

	Killed	Died of Wounds	Wounded to C.C.S	Remain at duty
Vimy Sector				1
Mont St. Eloy	12	4	11	5
Maroeuil	-	-	2	4
Cojeul River Area			12	4
Totals	12	4	25	14

Appendix VII   August 1918 War Diary

UNDERGROUND DRESSING STATION
FOURIE

Treleus Road

Marceuil Road

Appendix II
War Diary
August 1918.

Appx III
War Diary

DIAGRAM OF ROUTES OF EVACUATION

2ND AUGUST, 1918.

+   △   ◁|◁   ‖△   ——   - - -

+   R.A.P.
△   RELAY POST
◁|◁   MOTOR POINT
‖△   ENTRAINING POINT
——   LIGHT RAILWAY
- - -   ROAD.

DAY RAILHEAD, RIGHT BRANCH, CUTTING.
DAY RAILHEAD, LEFT BRANCH, DAYLIGHT.
NIGHT RAILHEAD, LEFT BRANCH, LONG WOOD

TO A.D.S. ON LEFT
POST TRENCH
FARBUS B.2.d.23. (4 men)
WILLERVAL B.9.a.8.9 (6 men)
POST TRENCH
TIRED AL.
LONG WOOD B.15.a.1.9 (4 men)
TUNNEL B.15.c.4.2. (10 men)
EMBANKMENT
BRIERLEY B.20.b.2.8 (4 men)
TOMMY AL.
BRIERLEY AL.
ZEHNER AL.
DAYLIGHT B.19.d.5.9 (2 men)
CUTTING B.27.a.3.8. (5 men)
GUN PITS B.27.d.37. (4 men)
No. 1 POST H.3.c.6.9.
SIDING
CHANTICLERE G.G.d.5.3. (4 men)
TO ROCLINCOURT

APPENDIX TO 184 Iny BDE DEFENCE SCHEME
EVACUATION OF SICK AND WOUNDED

Appx IV
Ayl War Diary
1918

FROM	TO	BY DAY	BY NIGHT
(a) LONGWOOD (B.15.a.9) R.A.P. and Bearer Relay Post	TUNNEL (B.15.c.4.2) R.A.P. and Bearer Relay Post.	By hand carriage along Blind Railway Embankment	By Light Railway to ROCLINCOURT Railway Terminus on request by Telephone from Railway Signal box to CONTROL at ROCLINCOURT.
(b) TUNNEL (B.15.C.4.2) R.A.P. and Bearer Relay Post *	BRIERLEY (B.20.b.2.8) Bearer Relay Post.	By hand carriage via TOMMY or OUSE ALLY.	
(c) BRIERLEY B.20.b.2.8 Bearer Relay Post.	RIDGE RAILHEAD and ROADHEAD (B.19.d.5.9.)	By hand carriage via ZERNER ALLY.	
(d) RIDGE RAILHEAD and ROADHEAD at B.19.d.5.9	DIVISIONAL A.D.S. at ECURIE A.20.a.7.6.	By motor Ambce car on request from RAILHEAD Signal Box to A.D.S. or as by night	
(e) ROCLINCOURT RAILWAY TERMINUS.	DITTO.	By motor ambce on request from Railway Terminus Signal Box to A.D.S. by Telephone	
(f) DIVISIONAL A.D.S. at ECURIE A.20.a.7.6.	DIVISIONAL M.D.S. at MARDEUIL L.4.a.6.6.	WOUNDED By Motor Ambce car at once. SICK. By Horsed Ambce Wagon at 10.30 a.m. 2.30 p.m.; at other times by Motor Ambce Car	By Motor Ambce

(1) Gases are collected in ROCLINCOURT and ECURIE areas by horsed or motor Ambce Wagons as required

(2) All relay posts are staffed as below and have ample supplies of reserve stretchers, blankets, Thomas' and other splints and dressings

BEARER RELAY POST.	No of O. RANKS.
LONGWOOD	6
TUNNEL	8
BRIERLEY	6
RIDGE	4
CUTTING	8

In addition a reserve of bearers is kept at DIVISIONAL A.D.S. and another at DIVISIONAL M.D.S.

N.B * An alternative route may be taken By hand carriage from TUNNEL (para b above) along behind embankment to CUTTING Bearer Relay Post at B.24.a.3 from whence trains run on request by day or night to ROCLINCOURT TERMINUS.

D Jobson /Col
Lieut. Col.
O.C. 2nd. Lowl Fd. Ambce,
R. A. M. CORPS. T.

5 Aug 1918

Evacuations from ADS to Corps MDS from 6pm on 23rd Aug to 12 noon on 25th August

Appendix V

Formation	Wounded		Gassed		Sick		Totals	
	O.	O.R	O.	O.R	O.	O.R	O.	O.R
52 Div	14	331	3	142		22	17	495
56 "	2	115		25		10	2	150
59 "				2		1	-	3
25 "			1	12			1	12
Guards "		4				1		5
Corps Troops								
Other Formations		6			1	23	1	29
P.O.W.		18						18
	16	474	4	181	1	57	21	712

Appendix VI

War Diary. August 1918.

Date		Location	Remarks
17.8.18	1/2nd L.F.A.		Unit marched to Gouy Servins
18/20.8.18	—"—		At GOUY SERVINS.
20/21.8.18	—"—	51c. L.2.c.3.6	Marched to "Y" Huts AGNEZ-LES-DUISANS leaving at 11 p.m.
21/23.8.18	—"—	—"—	At AGNEZ-LES-DUISANS.
23.8.18	—"—		Marched to BRETONCOURT leaving 1.30 am
	M.D.S.	61c R.15.b.63	⎫ Taken over from 2/3 N. Midland F.A.
	W.W.C.P	" R.29.d.27	⎬
	A.D.S.	51b M.31.b.1.8	⎭
24.8.18	M.D.S ⎰	" M.31.b.1.8	Moved later in day to —
	⎱	" S.11.c.88	
	A.D.S ⎧	" S.4.c.9.0	In sunken road BOISLEAU-AU-MONT- later
	⎪	" S.11.B.5.8	BOISLEUX-au-MARC. later —
	⎨	" T.7.B.2.4	BOIRY-BECQUERELLE. later —
	⎩	" T.1.c.8.5	BOIRY COPSE.
25.8.18	M.D.S	" S.11.c.8.9	Moved on account of shelling.
26.8.18	TRANSPORT LINES		BOISLEUX ST. MARC and moved later to
	M.D.S ⎰	" S.11.b.5.8	MDS moved later to
	⎱	" S.6.d.9.1	BOIRY BECQUERELLE.
	A.D.S	" T.2.b.9.3	At sunken road HENIN.
27.8.18	M.D.S ⎧	" S.6.d.9.1	Moved later to ADS position at
	⎨	" T.2.b.9.3	HENIN and later on to
	⎩	" T.5.c.3.9	
	A.D.S ⎧	" T.2.b.9.3	Sunken road HENIN and later at
	⎪	" T.5.c.3.9	and thence to
	⎨	" U.1.d.9.6	LEMON BRIDGE FONTAINE. and later at
	⎩	" T.6.b.0.6	when BDE "side-slipped" in HINDENBURG LINE.
	TRANSPORT LINES ⎰	" S.6.d.9.1	BOIRY BECQUERELLE. thence to —
	⎱	" T.5.c.3.9	and on a/c of shelling moved back to —
		" T.33.d.15.9.2	beside CEMETERY

Army Form C. 2118.

WAR DIARY
or
INTELLIGENCE SUMMARY.

(Erase heading not required.)

2 London Field Amb
Vol 56
14/3324

Confidential

War Diary
for
September 1918

2nd London F.A.

COMMITTEE FOR THE
MEDICAL HISTORY OF THE WAR

Army Form C. 2118.

WAR DIARY
or
INTELLIGENCE SUMMARY.
(Erase heading not required.)

Instructions regarding War Diaries and Intelligence Summaries are contained in F.S. Regs., Part II. and the Staff Manual respectively. Title pages will be prepared in manuscript.

Place	Date	Hour	Summary of Events and Information	Remarks and references to Appendices
CROISILLES. Sheet 51B.	1/9/18		"B" Section running A.D.S. at T 23 a. 4. 6. (sheet 51 B) Car relay posts at U/c 9.9 and at U 19 89 4 (sheet 51B). At noon whole unit concentrated at T 23 a 4 6 (sheet 51 B) 155 Inf Bde. attacked beyond BULLECOURT at 6.30 pm and gained objectives. "C" section commenced h.h-frogged over "B" section and established A.D.S. at U 20 d 9 4. (sheet 51B) and to assist in evacuation of wounded all Transport (mechanical and horsed) moved up to A.D.S. as road became passable. Numbers of wounded passed through from 6 pm to 6 am 2nd noon. 9 officers 169 OR. Sick 6 OR.	
	2/9/18	9.30 am	Whole unit moved up to A.D.S at U 20 d 9.4 (sheet 51B). "B" section ready to leap-frog over "C" and form A.D.S. beyond BULLECOURT. "A" section to assist at U 20 d 9.4. (51B) Divisional collecting post was established at U 21.d.1.2 (sheet 51B)	5/1
		11 am	Moved (Limber + motor) relay posts established at U 22 c 4.3 and U 27 d. 2. 6. (sheet 51B) Reconnoitred roads as below :— (1) HENDECOURT – LONGATTE road good.	5/1

WAR DIARY
INTELLIGENCE SUMMARY
(Erase heading not required.)

Army Form C. 2118.

Place	Date	Hour	Summary of Events and Information	Remarks and references to Appendices
			2) Road running SE through U26 no nucleos and will be for some days.	
			3) Road from U.22 c 4.3 to U.23 central nucleos for wheeled transport but can be used by bearers.	
			Road from U.16 d to U.23 central no bad.	
			4) Roads from U.27 d 2.6 and roads south of Bullecourt cross roads nucleos at present.	
		7.30pm	Established Walking Post at C.4 b 5.2. From this point Horsed Wagons conveyed wounded to car relay post which was established at U.27 d 2.6 and from thence taken to A.D.S. which was moved back 250 yards from R.E. dump at U.30 d 9.4, owing to hostile bombing the previous night.	
			Number of cases passed through A.D.S. from 6 am to 6 pm.	
			Officers OR	
			Wounded 14 114	
			Gassed 1 2	
			Sick 1 8	
			A.D.M.S. arranging to have roads repaired. This road running from U.27 d 2.6 to C.4 d 2.3 was good even for motors, but from C.4 d 2.3 to C.11 a 2.8 thence to C.5 c 5.8 and on to cross roads at C.5 a 6.6 or C.5 b 6.6 it requires repairing.	
	3/9/18		Number of cases passed through A.D.S. from 6pm on 2nd to 6am on 3rd.	
			Officers OR	
			Wounded 2 32	
			Gassed 1 14	

Army Form C. 2118.

WAR DIARY
or
INTELLIGENCE SUMMARY.
(Erase heading not required.)

Place	Date	Hour	Summary of Events and Information	Remarks and references to Appendices
	3/9/18	am 6.15	Wagon park established at C.5.a.6.6.	
		8.30	A.D.S established in QUEANT at C.12.b.5.9.	
		11.30	Headquarters on move to QUEANT. No casualties passing through A.D.S. which is in touch with all Bearer officers.	
		1pm	Whole unit arrived in QUEANT. having been delayed en route owing to road having been mined and blown up, and alternative roads in bad state of repair.	
		6pm	Division not in action having been "gassed out" by Guards Division and 63rd Division which have joined up. Number of cases passed through from 6am. 9 O.R. wounded 3 O.R. sick.	
		10pm	Heavy bombing round camps area, mostly to the right.	B/O
QUEANT	4/9/18		Enemy long range gun got into transport lines. Even tho' he horses were well scattered and tied to their wagons, 3 were killed & wounded & 2 light wounded. 1 Driver killed & 3 O.Rs too lightly wounded. About 6pm Transport lines were accordingly moved back to NOREUIL as whole valley has been under shell fire.	B/O

WAR DIARY
INTELLIGENCE SUMMARY.

Place	Date	Hour	Summary of Events and Information	Remarks and references to Appendices
NOREUIL C.10.c.9.1.	5/9/18	8 a.m.	A.D.S. & A.D.M.S. remained at QUEANT but as before are in reserve really - only a nucleus left, as the cross roads nearby are a special target. Collecting post also left at PRONVILLE.	S/S Sheet 57c
			Headquarters moved from QUEANT to NOREUIL (Sqr. C.10.c.9.1) A.D.S. remained at D.1.d central and collecting Post with car at D.9.b.2.2. Change of locations notified A.D.M.S. and three B.H.Q's, also Bde Bearer parties. Two more horses died of wounds, and 3 attached from 1/1st L.F.A. bolted from lines and not yet found. 2 unattached from 1/1st also bolted. Notified O.C. 1/1st of the occurrence. Very few casualties passed through during night of 4/5th Sept. Orders received to move back to BOISLEUX area, but these were cancelled later. Division in close corps support. One Brigade in front of BULLECOURT and other two just behind.	
	6/9/18		Warning wire received from A.D.M.S. to be prepared to take over Corps Main Dressing Stn by 12.00, but this was cancelled. O.C. attended conference at office of A.D.M.S. XVII Corps.	S/S S/S

WAR DIARY
or
INTELLIGENCE SUMMARY.
(Erase heading not required.)

Army Form C. 2118.

Place	Date	Hour	Summary of Events and Information	Remarks and references to Appendices
U.25.a.2.0	7/9/18	8 am	Division moved down into bivouac area round ECOUST and ST LEGER. Unit bivouac area occupied at U25 a 2.0. and exercised medical supervision of and collection of sick from 155th and 157th Inf Bdes. Slightly sick to be treated in Field Ambulance. "Dug-in" tents only means of shelter.	
	8/9/18	9.30	Kit inspection and re-organisation of sections and equipment.	5/p
		11.30	Church Parade.	
		1 pm	Camp Fatigues.	
		5 pm	Weather broke down. Heavy rain made it impossible for patients to be retained.	
	9/9/18		Heavy rain at intervals during whole of day. Very few sick passing through. Capt RODD to 54th Brigade RGA for duty.	5/p
	10/9/18		Weather rainy trek; sick very few in number	5/p
	11/9/18		Weather still stormy trek.	6/p
	12/9/18		Numbers of sick continue the very small; whilst Appx. showing numbers for 155th & 157th Inf Bgs. which are being collected daily by their M. Amb:s.	5/p

WAR DIARY
or
INTELLIGENCE SUMMARY.

Army Form C. 2118.

Place	Date	Hour	Summary of Events and Information	Remarks and references to Appendices
U25a 2.0 (Sheet 51 C)	Sept 1918	13th	Evacuations of sick very few in number. Weather still stormy & colder	S/P
"		14th	Weather better. 1Sgt. & 22 O.R's arrived as reinforcements. Awt'd 5 ORs Sheepkr.	S/P
"		15th	155th Inf. Bge. going into the line in relief of Bge. of 57th Div. this evening.	S/P
"		16th	157th Inf. Bge. going into the line in relief of Bge. of 57th Div. this evening. Capt. GOLDIE and Lt. She. heads Sub-dis' attacks of 157th Inf. Bge. from today for duty. Remainder of Amb'ce B.G. in reserve.	S/P
"		17th	Moved HdQrs forward about 1000 yds to S.E.@ 9 central (57C) afrof. Bearers Subdiv'r. sent forward to reinforce Bearers of 155th Inf. Bge. for 24 hours.	S/P
9 central Sheet 57C		18th	Weather stormy.	S/P
		19th	" " ; still in reserve.	S/P

WAR DIARY
or
INTELLIGENCE SUMMARY.
(Erase heading not required.)

Army Form C. 2118.

Place	Date	Hour	Summary of Events and Information	Remarks and references to Appendices
C Central	Sept/1918 20th		20 Bearers sent to 1/1st Lowland Fd Amble to reinforce Bearers of 156th Inf. Bge.	S/p
"	21st		Lt. W. G. R. ROSS reported as reinforcement bringing strength up to 5 medical officers.	S/p
"	22nd		20 Bearers still with Bge. in the Line. Others " on fatigues at Div. M.D.S.	S/p
"	23rd		Reconnaissance made of a Bge. front of E.D. Bn. to northern beyond BOURSIES and CAMBRAI-BAPAUME Road.	S/p
"	24th		Weather variable at times showery but usually dry, bright & crisp in the mornings.	S/p
"	25th		Sent B. Section tent sub-divn. to J.9.b.4.1 (sheet 57C) to form an A.D.S. in an L shaped piece of trench with dug outs & iron which can be salved with pappies from all round. By evening accommodation completes with two dressing rooms 10ft Square & underground covered trench accommodation for 2 doz.	S/p

WAR DIARY
or
INTELLIGENCE SUMMARY.

Army Form C. 2118.

Place	Date	Hour	Summary of Events and Information	Remarks and references to Appendices
E.9 central (57 C)	26"		lying cases. This position is 200 yds. W. of cross roads + 100 yards on N. side of road though perhaps near enough cross roads is well lighted as road screening and the ruined factory orchard all come between the site & BOURLON WOOD, + all sites beyond are in full view. B. section tent sub division marched off to A.D.S. at 6a.m. The evening accommodation was completed & whole ad. Class transport lines moves in by dusk. The Bearers meantime having joined Capn GOLDIE Bde-Bearer Officer at 157th Inf. Bde. H.Qrs. during the afternoon.	D/p
BERT ROOT FACTORY J.9.d.4.1. (2ed 57 C)	27"		Division attacked with 1st & 3rd Bdes. The Field Amb.s was allotted the duty of clearing the 157th Inf. Bde. + M.G. Battn whose objectives extended to the canal outside the BAPAUME CAMBRAI Road. Car Post established at zero on BOURSIES. At 8.30 a.m. Car Post moved to K1 & 87	D/p

WAR DIARY
or
INTELLIGENCE SUMMARY

Army Form C. 2118.

Place	Date	Hour	Summary of Events and Information	Remarks and references to Appendices
	Sept/18			
J98 41	28th		Horses, ambce wagons etc Coy MDS. beyond ECOUST during the day. one car has radiator burst by Shell fire at K.1.6.8.7 & another whose driver was killed at the wheel in BOURSIES has front axle bent. No casualties among R.A.M.C personnel Transport. Cars moved forward to J9.b.4.1. in sunken Total cases passed thro; ADS. this 24hours 160; about 100 ? own Brit.	S/P
	29th		Division is resting in held bivouacs on W. of canal. Cars kept open at K.1.6.8.7 & everyone is resting.	S/P
	30th		" " weather changeable	S/P
			— Div still resting but now under orders to move at 12 hrs notice.	S/P

D. Dobson Col.
Lieut. Col.
O.C. 2nd. Low. Fd. Amb.ce,
R.A.M. CORPS, T.

ADMS
52nd Division

Ref DOMS XVII Corps No 6/100
ADMS 52 Div No MO/192

Lessons learnt during the recent operation in the COJUL and SENSEE River areas and suggestions for improvements, organization and Equipment

Under Divisional Medical Arrangement

(A) A Bearer Officer and two bearer sub-divisions formed a Brigade Bearer Party and were attached to each Infantry Brigade

(B) 2nd Lowland Field Amb less this officer and two bearer sub-divisions reinforced by 4 extra horsed amb" wagons and 8 extra motor amb. cars "ran" the ADS and responsible for the evacuation from the Bde. Bearer Parties to the Corps MDS

Distribution of personnel - Methods of Working

A. O.i/c Bde. Bearer Parties attached at least 4 Bearers to each R A P and formed Bearer Relay Posts every 500 & 750 yds from R A P back to the furthest forward point to which horsed or mechanical transport could be pushed by O C 1/2 Lowland Field Amb

B. 1/2nd Lowland Field Amb was organised thus -

B) C Bearer sub-divisions were completed up to establishment with one officer only and formed the Bde Bearer party of 157th Inf Bde.

A B & C Tent sub divisions were completed up to Establishment (except that A had no officer)

A Headquarters Sub-divisions consisting of O C Sgt Major Orderly Room staff Q M S & OC's orderly and postman was formed

On completion of the above on account of casualties during the advance it was seen that a Section bearer sub-division could be spared

The effect of this subdivision was that B & C by-passed over each other as they formed & closed ADSs in the advance.

A was kept in reserve, was not used as an independent detachment, but throughout was broken up to reinforce B or C as required.

Mobilization Equipment was in very large part dumped and left with a guard.

The transport of each Tent Subdivision consisted of one water cart and one specially packed battle-A.D.S. limbered wagon containing the following food & equipment, having an attachment for 4 two-gallon petrol tins for water (vide Appendix I). There were thus two of these special wagons always ready to move forward & leapfrog over the existing ADS.

Headquarter Subdivision usually occupied the site of the recently closed-down ADS along with the personnel of that subdivision & also that of Ambulance Horsed and Mechanical transport were similarly divided into two echelons, a forward one consisting of one water cart, one battle-A.D.S. limbered wagon at ADS + 2, three or 4 amb^ce wagons or cars, the last-named being frequently pushed well forward even beyond the working ADS and well separated & concealed if possible, and a Headquarters one which usually accompanied the Fd Amb^ce HQrs as a whole.

Horsed Amb^ce wagons were frequently able before the roads were repaired to proceed a mile or so further forward than motor amb^ce cars and proved invaluable at times on this account.

P.T.O.

meantime consider that the formation of a large dump behind meets all requirements when warfare assumes a semi-mobile or mobile phase.

12/9/18.	D. Jobson Scott
	Lt Col.
	O.C. 1/2 Lowland F.A. Amb⁰

General classification

    A Medical Comforts
    B Surgical dressings Antiseptics Splints
    C Stretchers Blankets Ground Sheets
    D Kettles Stoves
    E Paraffin S V M

DETAILS

A Medical Comforts Pannier
    Tea 20 lbs   Oxo 12 lbs
    Sugar 40 lbs   Salt 2 lbs
    Milk 20 tins   Brandy 2 bottles

B Gauze * wool   1 bale
   Bandages   1 bale   200 Shell Dressings
   *Eusol   1 jar   200 First Field Dressings
   *Rysol   3 tubes   4 Thomas Splints Gooch
      and assorted splints

C Stretchers 12   Blankets 50
   Ground Sheets 60

D Camp Kettles 4   *Primus Stove 1   *Beatrice Stove 1
   1 Axe

E Paraffin (4 gallons) tins   S V M (1 pint) tin

H Pannier
   4 Hand Acetylene lamps * Carbide
   Roll of Instruments
   Sterilizer
   Towels   Enamelled tins 3 pints   Stomach warmer
   1 Enamel basin   12 tins   1 towel
   Soap 2 cas   nail brushes & scissors
   Candles   2 pails

* In summer

app I

Contents of Battle - A.D.S. Limbered Wagon.

1. Medical Comforts Pannier.

Tea 20 lbs.   Oxo 12 lbs.   Brandy 2 bottles
Sugar 40 lbs.   Salt 2 lbs.   2 cases (16 tins) Fancy Biscuits
Milk 40 tins.   10 lbs. Candles.

2. Dressings. Antiseptic. Splints etc.

Gauze   1 bale (1500 yds)   2 Surgical Haversacks
Wool   "   50 lbs.   2 Water Bottles
200 Shell Dressing   4 Thomas Splints (complete)
Bandages. 1 bale (1800. 3")   Gooch splinting & assorted splints
Eusol   1 jar.

3.

12 Stretchers.   50 Blankets.   60 Ground Sheets.

4. Camp Kettles 4.   Primus Stove. 1.   Beatrice Stove 1.
Operating Lamp 1.

5. Paraffin 2 (petrol) tins   S.V.M. 1 (petrol) tin
Carbide 30 lbs.   12 Tins Solidified alcohol.

H. Pannier

4 hand Acetylene lamps.   3 rolls Carbolized tow.
1 Sterilizer   2 Directing Flags
12 bowls.   2 A.T. Syringes
1 Enamel basin 15"   60 bottle A.T. Serum
2 Stomach Warmers.   6 rolls Adhesive Tape
2 Enamel feeders   1 Urinal
12 Towels.
2 bars Soap
2 nail brushes
1 pr Hair Clippers

Army Form C. 2118.

WAR DIARY
or
INTELLIGENCE SUMMARY.
(Erase heading not required.)

War Diary
for
October 1918.

1/2 no London Field Ambulance

149/5401

WAR DIARY or INTELLIGENCE SUMMARY.

Army Form C. 2118.

Place	Date	Hour	Summary of Events and Information	Remarks and references to Appendices
Sheet 57.C. J.9.6.6.4	6/27/18.	1st	Order to move & take over A.D.S. & posts from 63rd Div. arrived about 1100. A.D.S. at ANNEUX at once taken over & connected up to Amb. train. Car Post at F.28 d 5.9 taken over & connected at once into an A.D.S. & forward Car Post at F.29 b 4.6 also taken over & retained as such. At 5.40 p.m. before the med. relief has been completed 155th Inf. Bge. attacked in order to afford F'D. DE PARIS but failed. With 10 cars & 1 lorry all cases were all to be cleared by 2 a.m. 2nd Oct.	5/p
Sheet 57.C. F.25 a.3.5 ANNEUX		2nd	Car Post pushed forward to safer place out of brisk Head shelling to F.30 a.6.6. Summary of Casualties *	*app. 5/p
		3rd	Reconnaissance made towards RUMILLY in event of our advancing routes would thro' this village in all probability.	5/p
		4th	A.D.S. at CANTAING severely shelled for 6 hours, afternoon & evening, &	5/p

WAR DIARY or INTELLIGENCE SUMMARY.

Army Form C. 2118.

Place	Date	Hour	Summary of Events and Information	Remarks and references to Appendices
ANNEUX	30/11/8		accordingly during the night all cases were switched from Cav. Post rifly back to Quber H.Qrs. at ANNEUX which therefore acted as an A.D.S.	
		5ᵗʰ	A.D.S. received shelles this morn, advice being scores every 10 mins or so: A.D.S. itself. New site chosen in sunken road 600 yards back, & dugouts there cleared from temporary occupants who moved back to ANNEUX area. Brit. is coming out during the night.	S/P
		6ᵗʰ	Division relieved with line & Cav. Post closed at 6 a.m. Unit moved back after concentrating in the morning at ANNEUX, & Beetroot Factory at a 15.9642 DOIGNIES.	S/P

WAR DIARY
or
INTELLIGENCE SUMMARY.
(Erase heading not required.)

Army Form C. 2118.

Place	Date	Hour	Summary of Events and Information	Remarks and references to Appendices
J9 6 4 2 (DOIGNIES)	Oct/18	7th	Left camp at 3.30 p.m.; entrained at VAUX-VAUCOURT 6 p.m.; arrived next morning at 6 a.m. on	S/P
"		8th	unit at PETIT HOUVIN; eight hours late, & marched 10 miles or so to BLAVINCOURT Huts camp site, arriving about 10 a.m.	S/P
"		9th	Equipment is being completely overhauled. Unit is acting as a temporary D.R.S. for cases likely to be well within 4 days	S/P
"		10th	Unit is acting as a D.R.S.; weather mild but foggy.	S/P
"		11th	Weather foggy.	S/P

WAR DIARY
or
INTELLIGENCE SUMMARY.
(Erase heading not required.)

Army Form C. 2118.

Instructions regarding War Diaries and Intelligence Summaries are contained in F. S. Regs., Part II. and the Staff Manual respectively. Title pages will be prepared in manuscript.

Place	Date	Hour	Summary of Events and Information	Remarks and references to Appendices
	Oct.	12	The Commanding Officer, Lt. Col. D. JOBSON SCOTT went on short leave. Major D. LEWIS temporarily assuming command. 3 Reinforcements (other ranks) also reported from the base for duty. All the personnel of the Ambulance had hot spray baths in m/c the Hospital Huts. Some kitch bring received in connection with the works supply at the Divisional baths at LIGNEREUIL. All were examined by a M.O. but no cases of scabies were detected. All the men received clean change of underclothing. Orders received from ADMS to take down on a Divisional Rest Station, the duties to be taken over by the 1/1 LFA at QUATRE VENTS and a Skin Centre for Scabies cases at ESTRÉE CAUCHIE.	S/p
		13		S/p
		14	All personnel again had baths at GRAND = RULLECOURT.	S/p
		15	Regular Course of Physical & general R.T.M.C Training began.	S/p

WAR DIARY or INTELLIGENCE SUMMARY

Army Form C. 2118.

Place	Date	Hour	Summary of Events and Information	Remarks and references to Appendices
	1/6		Physical Sickness
Statement of Major Black & others.
During the past week 9.10.18 — 15.10.18 (inclusive) 63 patients were admitted to Hospital including 17 from units outside the 157 Bde.
These 23 were transferred to the 12th Stationary Hosp. St Pol — amongst which were 2 emr other mistns 1 Syphilis 1 Subacute Rheumatism 3 I.C.T. hand 1 Varicose veins 4 2 Lacerations for Gundson 1 defective vision 1 P.U.O. etc.
The other cases which were later retained discharged, Ruptured camps at MAZINGARBE n transferred to Divisional Rest Station at LES QUATRE VENTS. Consist mainly of Bronchitis, Rheumatism, debility, Influenza, Simple diarrhoea, Scabies, Scars D/H in all 8h.	

WAR DIARY
or
INTELLIGENCE SUMMARY.

Army Form C. 2118.

Place	Date	Hour	Summary of Events and Information	Remarks and references to Appendices
BLAVINCOURT	Oct /18	17th	Unit closing up as D.R.S.	S/1
"		18th	All patients, stores & wagons packed.	S/1
ST ELOY.		19th	Marches to ST ELOY	S/1
HENIN LIETARD P.25. sheet 44A		20th	Marches to HENIN LIETARD & took on Site of French Hosp¹ on P.25 C / 4 Sheet 44A. This has been used as a German Hosp¹ too but was in a deplorably untidy & filthy condition and all cellars (which communicates with itself & the lift the latter out of gear) were impregnated with mustard gas. Cellars were scaled up and arrival as huts & chloride of lime	S/1

WAR DIARY
or
INTELLIGENCE SUMMARY.
(Erase heading not required.)

Army Form C. 2118.

Place	Date	Hour	Summary of Events and Information	Remarks and references to Appendices
HENIN LIETARD	21st		freely sprinkled over the entrance seals, but basement could not be used. 20 gassed cases were admitted (mustard) during the night from a gas bomb which hap explosion. Twenty more mustard gas cases admitted from the Labour Co. who were clearing up after the explosion above mentioned. Subm^d floor completely cleaned out + used as an H.O.P. to detain only as journey to C.C.S. at OISANS takes 7 8 hours. O roads are very bad. C Section under Major BLACK accompanies 157 Inf. Bde. to just this side of DOUAI.	5/1
	22nd		Whole of upper floor entirely cleared out in billets to personnel a/c of gas + spec. Basement floor still unavailable. O/c unable to keep out the Gas, which is however largely sealed up + causes no trouble but finds its way into basement would probably clear the house cookhouse fc are I still outside. 170 patients in Hosp.	5/1

WAR DIARY or INTELLIGENCE SUMMARY

Army Form C. 2118.

Place	Date	Hour	Summary of Events and Information	Remarks and references to Appendices
HENIN-LIETARD			even tho' about 50 severely wounded, many moderately severely. Some cases had taken place. This Hosp¹ is also being used as a Relay post for all cases en route from front to clear at DOUAI, SANS etc, all of, to ensure that splints are well applied, patients are able to continue the journey, rechauffement is not necessary, or, dressing not disturbed. S.W. bots. are kept ready at all times for all patients anyone.	
	23ʳᵈ		Moved tons. to billets just this side of DOUAI. off hanging away hosp¹ with about 50 patients. f/1ˢᵗ pour 70. Amb: Fest Division of H. Div. (Stan Bn⁵. of /1ᵉʳ is with its Rgt. Group).	S/p
FLINES-LEZ-RACHES (R 23 See 44A)	24ᵗʰ		Moved with 157 Bgr. group to FLINES-LEZ-RACHES.	S/p

WAR DIARY
or
INTELLIGENCE SUMMARY.
(Erase heading not required.)

Army Form C. 2118.

Place	Date	Hour	Summary of Events and Information	Remarks and references to Appendices
FLINES	Oct/18 25th		Overhauling section equipment, market ∝.	S/p
"	26th		Unit resting.	S/p
LANDAS	27th		Unit moves to LANDAS (H.28.) Sheet 44 units Bde Group 157 & 8 Bdy	S/p
LECELLES	28th		" " LECELLES (I.28) " " " " "	S/p
			156th Inf. Bde. went into the line in relief — Bde of 12th Div. today units 11th Coml. Fr Auts " in Bde.g. ASS & 157th Inf Bde. 157th Inf Bde. is in LECELLES area in support & 1/2 Coml. Fr Auts is only partly opened up.	S/p
"	29th		Weather bright & fine. Reconnoitred possible sites for strong influenza Cases should an epidemic occur.	S/p
"	30th		Overhauling + cleaning up equipment	S/p
"	31st		Ditto.	S/p

D. Jobson/Col?/Col
OC 1/2 Coml Fr Auts

Summary of casualties passed thro A.D.S.

6 pm 1/10/18 to 6 am 2/10/18

	Wounded		Gassed		Sick	
	O's	OR's	O's	OR's	O's	OR's
52 Div	11	199	—	7	—	14
57 "	1	31	—	2	—	2
63 "	2	36	—	—	—	2
Corps Tps	1	8	—	—	—	—
P of W.	—	1	—	—	—	—
Totals.	15	275	—	9	—	18

6 am 2/10/18 to 6 pm 2/10/18

	Wounded		Gassed		Sick	
	O's	OR's	O's	OR's	O's	OR's
52 Div	—	46	—	2	—	19
57	—	3	—	—	—	—
63	—	—	—	—	—	6
Corps Tps	—	—	—	—	—	1
Totals	—	49	—	2	—	26

6pm 2/10/18 to 6am 3/10/18

	wounded		gassed		sick	
	Os	ORs	Os	ORs	Os	ORs
52 Div	1	28	—	—	1	3
57	—	1	—	—	—	—
63	—	2	—	—	—	—
Corps Tps	—	1	—	—	—	—
Totals	1	32	—	—	1	3

6am 3/10/18 to 6am 4/10/18

	wounded		gassed		sick	
	Os	ORs	Os	ORs	Os	ORs
52 Div	1	39	—	1	1	26
3 Div	—	3	—	—	—	—
Corps	—	8	—	—	1	6
Totals	1	50	—	1	2	32

From 6 A.M. on 4/10/18 to 6 A.M. on 5/10/18.

	Wounded		Gassed		Sick	
	Off.	O.R.	Off.	O.R.	Off.	O.R.
52 Div	1	33	-	1	4	22
57 "	-	6	-	-	-	1
63 "	-	1	-	-	-	-
Corps Troops	-	6	-	1	-	4
	1	46	-	2	4	27

From 6 A.M. on 5/10/18 to 6 A.M. 6/10/18

	Off	O.R.	Off	O.R.	Off	O.R.
52 Div	-	19	-	-	-	21
57 "	-	-	-	1	-	12
Corps Troops	-	8	-	2	-	9
	-	27	-	3	-	42

Army Form C. 2118.

WAR DIARY
of
INTELLIGENCE SUMMARY.
(Erase heading not required.)

Confidential
War Diary
November 1918.
1/2nd Low. Fld. Amb CE

Place	Date	Hour	Summary of Events and Information	Remarks and references to Appendices

Instructions regarding War Diaries and Intelligence Summaries are contained in F. S. Regs., Part II. and the Staff Manual respectively. Title pages will be prepared in manuscript.

WAR DIARY
or
INTELLIGENCE SUMMARY.

Army Form C. 2118.

Place	Date	Hour	Summary of Events and Information	Remarks and references to Appendices
LE SELLES I. 29 (sheet 44)	Nov/18	1st	2 Cables is still in reserve. There is very little doing on the front. All equipment is being thoroughly overhauled. Some of the drivers & wheelmen have been started all front line running subjects.	A/I
"	2nd		Weather continues mild but showery at times.	A/I
"	3rd		Weather showery.	A/I
"	4th		Weather variable. Ambce still in reserve.	A/I
"	5th		In preparation for entering the line again site of an ADS chosen at HAUTE RIVE. (J36.c.0.9. sheet 44)	A/I
"	6th		Reconnaissance made of roads in front of HAUTE RIVE & down to river made as weather very wet & visibility very poor.	A/I
"	7th		Reconnaissance continued. as roads are very poor in parts.	A/I
"	8th		Moved to HAUTE RIVE & opened an A.D.S. there but roads & area this evening occurred a mire impassable today.	A/I

WAR DIARY or INTELLIGENCE SUMMARY

Army Form C. 2118.

Place	Date	Hour	Summary of Events and Information	Remarks and references to Appendices
HAUTERIVE J36c a9 Sheet 44	Nov/18 9th		Moved behind 157 & 156 Inf. Bges. keeping in touch with both via BONSECOURS. Keeping the second Canal over amateur-curtain made bridge at BLATON & cottages on other side of canal in GRAND BRUYERE where ADS established but we were not in contact with the retreating enemy yet.	D/1
GRAND BRUYERE G9d91	10th		Moved with 156 Bge. (157 being accompanied by /3 Lou.t. Fd (Amb) to SIRAULT (I 1.6.5.9) where ADS. established, enemy encountered in front & about 70 casualties dealt with. These were retained till next morning as route to VALENCIENNES (the furthest forward C.C.S.) was so difficult even by day.	
	11th		ADS. established VALCROSSE, road routes reconnoitred & car posts established in front of ambulances & Cases evacuated from SIRAULT.	D/1

Army Form C. 2118.

WAR DIARY
or
INTELLIGENCE SUMMARY.
(Erase heading not required.)

Instructions regarding War Diaries and Intelligence Summaries are contained in F. S. Regs., Part II. and the Staff Manual respectively. Title pages will be prepared in manuscript.

Place	Date	Hour	Summary of Events and Information	Remarks and references to Appendices
VACRESSE C.30.c.6.4 Sheet 45	12th		After which arriver moves reserves to divence 11am. + HQrs. moved to A.D.S. at VACRESSE (C.30.c.6.4) Sheet 45. Unit resting.	DD
	13th		Moved to ERBISOEUL to concentrate in Bge front area (D.27.d.8.8 Sheet 45).	DD
ERBISOEUL	14th		All equipment being overhauled + paint + polish renewed. Weather glorious - hard frost	DD
"	15th		" " - Unit polishing & cleaning up.	DD
"	16th		" " " "	DD
"	17th		" " " "	DD
"	18th		" more cloudy + not so frosty.	DD
"	19th		" foggy + cold. Unit drilling ½ hours a day.	DD
"	20th		" " . Educational scheme of lectures + discussions every second evening started.	DD
"	21st		Weather milder & bright	DD

Army Form C. 2118.

WAR DIARY
or
INTELLIGENCE SUMMARY.
(Erase heading not required.)

Instructions regarding War Diaries and Intelligence Summaries are contained in F. S. Regs., Part II. and the Staff Manual respectively. Title pages will be prepared in manuscript.

Place	Date	Hour	Summary of Events and Information	Remarks and references to Appendices
ERBISOEUIL	22nd		Cool bright weather	5/1
	23rd		" " Ceremonial Inspection of 157th Bde by Bde	5/1
			Group by 157 Bde. Bde Group Commander, Bryn. PRICE.	5/1
	24th		Weather bright. Cusop swam.	
	25th		Weather mild	
	26th		Programme of training in morning and	5/1
	27th		Educational training in afternoons.	
	28th			
	29th			
	30th		D. Edmond Cott	5/1
			Lt Col	
			OC 6th Lowland 77 Amb.	

Army Form C. 2118.

WAR DIARY
or
INTELLIGENCE SUMMARY.
(Erase heading not required.)

Confidential
War Diary
of
1/2nd Lowland F.A.

from 1st Decr 1918 to 31st Decr 1918
Volume No. 43

COMMITTEE FOR THE MEDICAL HISTORY OF THE WAR
Date 4 JUL 1919

1/2nd LOWLAND FIELD AMBULANCE.

140/34/51

Army Form C. 2118.

WAR DIARY
or
INTELLIGENCE SUMMARY
(Erase heading not required.)

Instructions regarding War Diaries and Intelligence Summaries are contained in F. S. Regs., Part II. and the Staff Manual respectively. Title pages will be prepared in manuscript.

Place	Date Decr	Hour	Summary of Events and Information	Remarks and references to Appendices
Mons Railway Station	1st	0700	Unit less 'B' Section Sub Division moved to MONS Railway Station at 0700 to receive returning refugees and Prisoners of War. The station was in a filthy and untidy condition, and personnel were put on to clean it up. 'B' Section Sub Division after evacuating all patients at ERBISOEUL moved to GHLIN to look after sick of 157th g.f. Bde. Group.	S/D
"	2nd		Station still being cleaned. Number of meals issued to refugees for 24 hrs. ending 0900 — 258 do. do. P.O.W. — 267 British do. do. do. — 108 French	S/D
"	3rd		Number of sick evacuated to No.1 C.C.S. MONS — {Lying 50, Sitting 400} from Ambulance 3 train. Number of meals issued to refugees for 24 hrs ending 0900 — 2,509 do. do. P.O.W. — 92 British do. do. do. — 697 French do. do. do. — 76 Italian	S/D

WAR DIARY

INTELLIGENCE SUMMARY.

(Erase heading not required.)

Army Form C. 2118.

Place	Date	Hour	Summary of Events and Information	Remarks and references to Appendices
Mons Railway Station	4		Number of meals issued to refugees for 24 hrs ending 0900 – 638 do do do do – 58 British do do do do – 203 French P.O.W. Number of sick evacuated to No 1 C.C.S. MONS from Ambulance { Lying 150, Sitting 380 } train. 740 Iron Rations were put on train with refugees proceeding to DOUAI. 764 refugees on board train.	S/D
"	5		Number of meals issued to refugees for 24 hrs ending 0900 – 3062 do do do do – 43 British P.O.W. do do do do – 110 French Number of patients evacuated from Ambulance trains to No 1 C.C.S. MONS – Sitting 318 do do do 4/3 Can. Fd. Amb. " – 12.5	S/D
"	6		Number of meals issued to refugees for 24 hrs ending 0900 – 5761 Number of patients evacuated from Ambulance train to No 1 C.C.S. MONS { Lying 132, Sitting 299 } do do do 1/3 Can. Fd. Amb. Sitting 130	S/D

Army Form C. 2118.

WAR DIARY
or
INTELLIGENCE SUMMARY.
(Erase heading not required.)

Place	Date	Hour	Summary of Events and Information	Remarks and references to Appendices
Mons Railway Station	7"		Number of meals issued to refugees for 24 hrs ending 0900 – 6593. Two trains left for DOUAI with 1580 refugees on board.	S/P
"	8"		Number of meals issued to refugees for 24 hrs. ending 0900 – 4069. Number of sick evacuated from Ambulance trains to No. 201 C.C.S., MONS { Officers Lying 11, Sitting 6; O. Ranks Lying 105, Sitting 419 }	S/P
"	9"		Number of meals issued to refugees for 24 hrs ending 0900 – 6503. Number of iron rations put on train of refugees for DOUAI – 935. 70 of refugees on board 707.	S/P
"	10"		Number of meals issued to refugees for 24 Hrs. ending 0900 – 7234. Number of sick evacuated from Ambulance trains to No. 1 C.C.S., MONS { Officers Lying 3, Sitting 9; O.E. Sitting 130 } do. No 4 Con. C.C.S, MONS { Officers Lying 6, Sitting 52; O. Ranks Sitting 251 }	S/P
"	11"		Number of meals issued to refugees for 24 Hrs. ending 0900 – 10,555. Two trains left with refugees for VALENCIENNES with 1658 men rations on board. do. Three trains do. DOUAI 2461 do. Number of sick evacuated from Amber trains to No. 1 C.C.S, MONS { Lying Officers 2, Sitting 2; O. Ranks Lying 147, Sitting 461 }	S/P

Army Form C. 2118.

WAR DIARY
or
INTELLIGENCE SUMMARY.
(Erase heading not required.)

Instructions regarding War Diaries and Intelligence Summaries are contained in F. S. Regs., Part II. and the Staff Manual respectively. Title pages will be prepared in manuscript.

Place	Date	Hour	Summary of Events and Information	Remarks and references to Appendices
Mons Railway Station	12		Number of meals issued to refugees for 24 hrs ending 0900 — 14,688 2,026 iron rations put on train with 2,022 refugees for VALENCIENNES. — 1919 do. 2,082 do. DOUAI	A/1
"	13		Number of meals issued to refugees for 24 hrs. ending 0900 — 12,417. 1,700 iron rations put on board train with 1644 refugees for VALENCIENNES. 1,698 do. 1746 do. DOUAI.	A/2
"	14		Number of meals issued to refugees for 24 hrs. ending 0900 — 9,767 Number of patients evacuated to 70th Can. C.C.S from 70¹ Amb: train { Officers 6, O. Ranks 172 do. 1/3ʳᵈ Lois. Fd. Amb. do. O. Ranks 360 Number of iron rations put on train of refugees for DOUAI — 636 for 679 refugees do. do. VALENCIENNES 620 " 1252 "	A/3
"	15		Number of meals issued to refugees for 24 hrs. ending 0900 — 9,548 Number of iron rations put on train of refugees for VALENCIENNES — 743 for 700 refugees do. do. DOUAI — 623 " 588 "	A/4

Army Form C. 2118.

WAR DIARY
or
INTELLIGENCE SUMMARY.
(Erase heading not required.)

Instructions regarding War Diaries and Intelligence Summaries are contained in F. S. Regs., Part II. and the Staff Manual respectively. Title pages will be prepared in manuscript.

Place	Date	Hour	Summary of Events and Information	Remarks and references to Appendices
Mons Railway Station	16"		Number of meals issued to refugees for 24 hrs. ending 0900 – 5,875 928 iron rations put on train with 930 refugees for VALENCIENNES. 496 " " " " 500 " " DOUAI.	CES
"	17"		Number of meals issued to refugees for 24 hrs. ending 0900 – 4,375 743 iron rations put on train with 690 refugees for VALENCIENNES. 550 " " " " 462 do. DOUAI. Now that the trains are running regularly, the figures will be a little more accurate.	CES
"	18"		Number of meals issued to refugees for 24 hrs. ending 0900 – 6,742 621 iron rations put on train with 574 refugees for VALENCIENNES. 1192 " " " " 1317 do. DOUAI. Lt. Col. SCOTT left for 14 days leave in U.K.	CES
"	19"		Number of meals issued to refugees for 24 hrs. ending 0900 – 7,866 1163 iron rations put on train with 1069 refugees for VALENCIENNES. 1020 " " " " 952 do. DOUAI.	CES

Army Form C. 2118.

WAR DIARY
or
INTELLIGENCE SUMMARY.
(Erase heading not required.)

Instructions regarding War Diaries and Intelligence Summaries are contained in F. S. Regs., Part II. and the Staff Manual respectively. Title pages will be prepared in manuscript.

Place	Date	Hour	Summary of Events and Information	Remarks and references to Appendices
Mons Railway Station	20th		Number of meals issued to refugees for 24 hrs ending 0900 – 3885. 1056 iron rations put on trains with 1157 refugees for DOUAI. 1012 do 893 do VALENCIENNES	CSS
"	21st		Number of meals issued to refugees for 24 hrs ending 0900 – 4,788. 892 iron rations put on train with 635 refugees for VALENCIENNES 882 do do DOUAI.	CSS
"	22nd		Number of meals issued to refugees for 24 hrs. ending 0900 – 5,691. 1,234 iron rations put on train with 1234 refugees for DOUAI. 963 do do VALENCIENNES.	CSS
"	23rd		Number of meals issued to refugees for 24 hrs ending 0900 – 5,384. 950 iron rations put on trains with 1,100 refugees for DOUAI. 973 do do VALENCIENNES.	CSS
"	24th		Number of meals issued to refugees for 24 hrs ending 0900 – 4,967. 1000 iron rations put on trains with 1,000 refugees for DOUAI. 537 do do VALENCIENNES.	CSS

WAR DIARY
or
INTELLIGENCE SUMMARY.
(Erase heading not required.)

Army Form C. 2118.

Place	Date	Hour	Summary of Events and Information	Remarks and references to Appendices
Mons Railway Station	25th		Number of meals issued to refugees for 24 hrs. ending 0900 — 4510. Iron rations put on train with refugees for DOUAI. do. VALENCIENNES.	C153
"	26th		Number of meals issued to refugees for 24 hrs. ending 0900 — 6,672. 1990 iron rations put on train with 1990 refugees for DOUAI. 7,it do. do. VALENCIENNES.	C152
"	27th		Number of meals issued to refugees for 24 hrs. ending 0900 — 7140. 1697 iron rations put on train with 697 refugees for DOUAI. 1448 do. do. VALENCIENNES.	C153
"	28th		Number of meals issued to refugees for 24 hrs. ending 0900 — 5154. 839 iron rations put on train with 839 refugees for DOUAI. 625 do. do. VALENCIENNES.	C153
"	29th		Number of meals issued to refugees for 24 hrs. ending 0900 — 3964. 870 iron rations put on train with 870 refugees for DOUAI. 1033 do. do. VALENCIENNES.	C153

Army Form C. 2118.

WAR DIARY
or
INTELLIGENCE SUMMARY.
(Erase heading not required.)

Instructions regarding War Diaries and Intelligence Summaries are contained in F. S. Regs., Part II. and the Staff Manual respectively. Title pages will be prepared in manuscript.

Place	Date	Hour	Summary of Events and Information	Remarks and references to Appendices
Reluy Station	30th		Number of meals issued to refugees for 24 hrs ending 0900 - 14162 632 iron rations put on train with 632 refugees for DOUAI 764 do. do. do. VALENCIENNES	C.S.2
	31st		Number of meals issued to refugees for 24 hrs ending 0900 - 15936 950 iron rations put on train with 950 refugees for DOUAI 858 do. do. do. VALENCIENNES	C.S.3

C S Blank Major
O.C. 2nd. Low Fd. Ambce
R. A. M. CORPS. T.

Army Form C. 2118.

52 Div
Box 249

140/3490

WAR DIARY
or
INTELLIGENCE SUMMARY.

(Erase heading not required.)

Confidential
War Diary
of
1/2nd Lowland F.A.
(2nd Scottish) N.O. 44

From 1st Jany. to 31st Jany. 1919

1/2nd LOWLAND
FIELD
AMBULANCE.

COMMITTEE FOR THE
MEDICAL HISTORY OF THE WAR
10 MAR 1919
Date

Instructions regarding War Diaries and Intelligence
Summaries are contained in F. S. Regs., Part II.
and the Staff Manual respectively. Title pages
will be prepared in manuscript.

Summary of Events and Information

Place	Date	Hour		Remarks and references to Appendices
	Jan 1919			

Army Form C. 2118.

WAR DIARY
or
INTELLIGENCE SUMMARY.
(Erase heading not required.)

Place	Date	Hour	Summary of Events and Information	Remarks and references to Appendices
MON Rly. Station	Jany 1919 1st		Number of meals issued to refugees for 24 hrs ending 0900 – 5949 988 iron rations put on train with 988 refugees for VALENCIENNES. 964 do do DOUAI.	C.C.S.
"	2nd		Number of meals issued to refugees for 24 hrs. ending 0900 – 3632 493 iron rations put on train with 493 refugees for VALENCIENNES. 487 do do DOUAI.	C.C.S.
"	3rd		Number of meals issued to refugees for 24 hrs ending 0900 – 3759 552 iron rations put on train with 552 refugees for VALENCIENNES. 496 do do DOUAI.	C.C.S.
"	4th		Number of meals issued to refugees for 24 hrs. ending 0900 – 3402 592 iron rations put on train with 592 refugees for VALENCIENNES. 863 do do DOUAI.	C.C.S.
"	5th		Number of meals issued to refugees for 24 hrs ending 0900 – 2633 459 iron rations put on train with 459 refugees for VALENCIENNES. 552 do do DOUAI.	C.C.S.

Army Form C. 2118.

WAR DIARY
or
INTELLIGENCE SUMMARY.
(Erase heading not required.)

Place	Date	Hour	Summary of Events and Information	Remarks and references to Appendices
Mons Rly Station	1919 6"		Number of meals issued to refugees for 24 hrs ending 0900 – 2860. 398 iron rations put on train with 398 refugees for VALENCIENNES. 326 do. do. do. DOUAI. Lt Col D. Gibson Scott returned from leave.	A52
"	7"		Number of meals issued to refugees for 24 hrs ending 0900 – 2148. 184 iron rations put on train with 481 refugees for VALENCIENNES. 495 do. do. do. DOUAI.	5/1
"	8"		Number of meals issued to refugees for 24 hrs ending 0900 – 4169. 392 iron rations put on train with 392 refugees for VALENCIENNES. 996 do. do. do. DOUAI.	5/1
"	9"		Number of meals issued to refugees for 24 hrs ending 0900 – 4135. 841 iron rations put on train with 841 refugees for VALENCIENNES. 849 do. do. do. DOUAI.	5/1
"	10"		Number of meals issued to refugees for 24 hrs ending 0900 – 4943. 1,110 iron rations put on train with 1,110 refugees for VALENCIENNES. 845 do. do. do. DOUAI.	5/1

Army Form C. 2118.

WAR DIARY
or
INTELLIGENCE SUMMARY.
(Erase heading not required.)

Place	Date 1919	Hour	Summary of Events and Information	Remarks and references to Appendices
Mons Rly. Station	11"		Number of meals issued to refugees for 24 hrs. ending 0900 - 2,260. 251 iron rations put on trains with 251 refugees for VALENCIENNES. 457 do. do. DOUAI.	S/1
	12"		Number of meals issued to refugees for 24 hrs. ending 0900 - 2,375. 314 iron rations put on trains with 314 refugees for VALENCIENNES. 843 do. do. DOUAI.	S/1
	13"		Number of meals issued to refugees for 24 hrs. ending 0900 - 2,132. 355 iron rations put on trains with 355 refugees for VALENCIENNES. 616 do. do. DOUAI.	S/1
	14"		Number of meals issued to refugees for 24 hrs. ending 0900 - 1,566. 335 iron rations put on trains with 335 refugees for VALENCIENNES. 698 do. do. DOUAI.	S/1
	15"		Number of meals issued to refugees for 24 hrs. ending 0900 - 1,989. 435 iron rations put on trains with 435 refugees for VALENCIENNES. 635 do. do. DOUAI.	S/1

Army Form C. 2118.

WAR DIARY
or
INTELLIGENCE SUMMARY.
(Erase heading not required.)

Place	Date 1919	Hour	Summary of Events and Information	Remarks and references to Appendices
Mons Rly Station	Jan. 16th		Number of meals issued to refugees for 24 hrs. ending 0900 – 1967. 442 iron rations put on board with 442 refugees for VALENCIENNES. 400 do. do. DOUAI.	S/1
	17th		Number of meals issued to refugees for 24 hrs. ending 0900 – 1567. 246 iron rations put on train with 246 refugees for VALENCIENNES. do. do. DOUAI.	S/1
	18th		Number of meals issued to refugees for 24 hrs. ending 0900 – 2585. 392 iron rations put on train with 392 refugees for VALENCIENNES. 572 do. do. DOUAI.	S/1
	19th		Number of meals issued to refugees for 24 hrs. ending 0900 – 2603. 422 iron rations put on train with 422 refugees for VALENCIENNES. 672 do. do. DOUAI.	S/1
	20th		Number of meals issued to refugees for 24 hrs. ending 0900 – 1710. 281 iron rations put on train with 281 refugees for VALENCIENNES. 500 do. do. DOUAI.	S/1

Army Form C. 2118.

WAR DIARY
or
INTELLIGENCE SUMMARY.
(Erase heading not required.)

Instructions regarding War Diaries and Intelligence Summaries are contained in F. S. Regs., Part II. and the Staff Manual respectively. Title pages will be prepared in manuscript.

Place	Date	Hour	Summary of Events and Information	Remarks and references to Appendices
Mons Rly Station	Jan 1919 21st		Number of meals issued to refugees for 24 hrs. ending 0900 – 1958. 281 iron rations put on train with 281 refugees for VALENCIENNES. 629 do. do. DOUAI.	S/1
	22nd		Number of meals issued to refugees for 24 hrs. ending 0900 – 1194. 267 iron rations put on train with 267 refugees for VALENCIENNES. 280 do. do. DOUAI.	S/1
	23rd		Number of meals issued to refugees for 24 hrs. ending 0900 – 2950. 637 iron rations put on train with 637 refugees for VALENCIENNES. 260 do. do. DOUAI.	S/1
	24th		Number of meals issued to refugees for 24 hrs. ending 0900 – 2231. 227 iron rations put on train with 227 refugees for VALENCIENNES. 475 do. do. DOUAI.	S/1
	25th		Number of meals issued to refugees for 24 hrs. ending 0900 – 1320. 168 iron rations put on train with 168 refugees for VALENCIENNES. 310 do. do. DOUAI.	S/1
	26th		Number of meals issued to refugees for 24 hrs. ending 0900 – 1304. 549 iron rations put on train with 549 refugees for VALENCIENNES. 824 do. do. DOUAI.	S/1

WAR DIARY
or
INTELLIGENCE SUMMARY.
(Erase heading not required.)

Army Form C. 2118.

Place	Date	Hour	Summary of Events and Information	Remarks and references to Appendices
Mons Rly Station	Sept 1919 27th		Number of meals issued to refugees for 24 hrs. ending 0900 - 1497. 326 iron rations put on the DOUAI-VALENCIENNES train with 326 refugees.	S/1
	28th		Number of meals issued to refugees for 24 hrs. ending 0900 - 1212. 377 iron rations put on the DOUAI-VALENCIENNES train with 377 refugees.	S/1
	29th		Number of meals issued to refugees for 24 hrs. ending 0900 - 650. 374 iron rations put on the DOUAI-VALENCIENNES train with 374 refugees.	S/1
	30th		Number of meals issued to refugees for 24 hrs. ending 0900 - 632. 280 iron rations put on the DOUAI-VALENCIENNES train with 280 refugees	S/1
	31st		Number of meals issued to refugees for 24 hrs. ending 0900 - 876. 280 iron rations put on the DOUAI-VALENCIENNES train with 280 refugees.	S/1

1219.

D. Dobson Capt.
RAMC
O.C. 1/2 Howland Fd. Amb.

Army Form C. 2118

WAR DIARY
or
INTELLIGENCE SUMMARY.

(Erase heading not required.)

War Diary
for
Month of February 1919.

1/2nd Ireland F.A.

Volume No 5

1/2 how and End

J.S.M

1/2nd Ireland F.A.

Army Form C. 2118.

WAR DIARY
or
INTELLIGENCE SUMMARY.
(Erase heading not required.)

Instructions regarding War Diaries and Intelligence Summaries are contained in F. S. Regs., Part II. and the Staff Manual respectively. Title pages will be prepared in manuscript.

Place	Date	Hour	Summary of Events and Information	Remarks and references to Appendices
Mons Rly. Station	February 1st		Number of meals issued to refugees for 24 hrs. ending 0900 – 657. 481 iron rations put on DOUAI–VALENCINNES train with 481 refugees.	S/1
	2nd		Number of meals issued to refugees for 24 hrs. ending 0900 – 564. 400 iron rations put on DOUAI–VALENCINNES train with 400 refugees.	S/1
	3rd		Number of meals issued to refugees for 24 hrs. ending 0900 – 983. 275 iron rations put on DOUAI–VALENCINNES train with 275 refugees.	S/1
	4th		Number of meals issued to refugees for 24 hrs. ending 0900 – 804. 431 iron rations put on DOUAI–VALENCINNES train with 431 refugees.	S/1
	5th		Number of meals issued to refugees for 24 hrs. ending 0900 – 975. 489 iron rations put on DOUAI–VALENCINNES train with 489 refugees.	S/1
	6th		Number of meals issued to refugees for 24 hrs. ending 0900 – 751. 533 iron rations put on DOUAI–VALENCINNES train with 533 refugees.	S/1
	7th		Number of meals issued to refugees for 24 hrs. ending 0900 – 717. 328 iron rations put on DOUAI–VALENCINNES train with 328 refugees.	S/1

Army Form C. 2118.

WAR DIARY
or
INTELLIGENCE SUMMARY.
(Erase heading not required.)

Instructions regarding War Diaries and Intelligence Summaries are contained in F. S. Regs., Part II. and the Staff Manual respectively. Title pages will be prepared in manuscript.

Place	Date	Hour	Summary of Events and Information	Remarks and references to Appendices
Mons Rly. Station	February 8th		Number of meals issued to refugees for 24 hrs. ending 0900 - 762. 364 iron rations put on DOUAI-VALENCINNES train with 364 refugees.	S/1
	9th		Number of meals issued to refugees for 24 hrs. ending 0900 - 780. 434 iron rations put on DOUAI-VALENCINNES train with 434 refugees.	S/1
	10th		Number of meals issued to refugees for 24 hrs. ending 0900 - 545. 305 iron rations put on DOUAI-VALENCINNES train with 305 refugees.	S/1
	11th		Number of meals issued to refugees for 24 hrs. ending 0900 - 335 iron rations put on DOUAI-VALENCINNES train with 335 refugees. Number of patients put on to Ambulance Train 26 February 1915. from 30th C.C.S. Officers {Lying 1, Sitting 1} O.Ranks {Lying 26, Sitting 51} from 1st C.C.S. Officers {Lying 1, Sitting 6} O.Ranks {Lying 54, Sitting 126}	S/1

Army Form C. 2118.

WAR DIARY
or
INTELLIGENCE SUMMARY.
(Erase heading not required.)

Instructions regarding War Diaries and Intelligence Summaries are contained in F.S. Regs., Part II. and the Staff Manual respectively. Title pages will be prepared in manuscript.

Place	Date July	Hour	Summary of Events and Information	Remarks and references to Appendices
Mons Rly Station	12"		Number of meals issued to refugees for 24 hrs ending 0900 – 544. 410 iron rations put on DOUAI-VALENCIENNES train with 410 refugees. On instructions from D.D.M.S., XXII Corps a "Halte Repas" was opened on the W. side of MONS Railway Station. 43 men were attached to this unit from 167" & 3rd Bde, 56th Division for work at the "Halte Repas". 3 Rs first Demobilization Train (New Zealanders) arrived at 3 pm with about 1200 on board. Soup, tea, bread, jam and cheese was issued to an orderly from each coach. (See Appendix "Organisation of XXII Corps Halte Repas at MONS").	S/1
"	13"		Number of meals issued to refugees for 24 hrs ending 0900 – 452. 304 iron rations put on DOUAI-VALENCIENNES train with 304 refugees.	S/1
"	14"		Number of meals issued to refugees for 24 hrs ending 0900 – 608. 220 iron rations put on DOUAI-VALENCIENNES train with 220 refugees. At 3 a.m. a Demobilization Train arrived with 1000 Canadians. Hot meals were issued to all. Another Canadian Demobilization Train arrived at 10 pm with about 1200 on board. Hot meals were ready and issued to the men.	S/1
"	15"		Number of meals issued to refugees for 24 hrs ending 0900 – 565. 118 iron rations put on board DOUAI-VALENCIENNES train with 118 refugees.	S/1

Army Form C. 2118.

WAR DIARY
or
INTELLIGENCE SUMMARY.
(Erase heading not required.)

Instructions regarding War Diaries and Intelligence Summaries are contained in F.S. Regs., Part II. and the Staff Manual respectively. Title pages will be prepared in manuscript.

Place	Date 1918	Hour	Summary of Events and Information	Remarks and references to Appendices
Mons Rly Station	Feby 16th		Number of meals issued to refugees for 24 hrs. ending 0900 - 350. 117 iron rations put on DOUAI-VALENCIENNES train with 117 refugees.	S/P
	17"		Number of meals issued to refugees for 24 hrs. ending 0900 - 125. 67 iron rations put on DOUAI-VALENCIENNES train with 67 refugees.	S/P
	18"		Number of meals issued to refugees for 24 hrs. ending 0900 - 610. 261 iron rations put on DOUAI-VALENCIENNES train with 261 refugees. At 3 p.m. our Demobilisation train of Australians came in, all the men being fed as usual.	S/P
	19"		Number of meals issued to refugees for 24 hrs. ending 0900 - 770. 200 iron rations put on DOUAI-VALENCIENNES train with 200 refugees.	S/P
	20"		Number of meals issued to refugees for 24 hrs. ending 0900 - 304. — iron rations put on DOUAI-VALENCIENNES train with — refugees. Number of patients put on Ambulance train 702 from 30th C.C.S. from 701 C.C.S. Officers {Lying 6, Sitting 5} O.R {Lying 66, Sitting 172} Officers {Lying 3, Sitting 1} O.R. {Lying 53, Sitting 44}	S/P

Army Form C. 2118.

WAR DIARY
or
INTELLIGENCE SUMMARY.
(Erase heading not required.)

Instructions regarding War Diaries and Intelligence Summaries are contained in F. S. Regs., Part II. and the Staff Manual respectively. Title pages will be prepared in manuscript.

Place	Date	Hour	Summary of Events and Information	Remarks and references to Appendices
Mons Rly Station	July 21.		Number of meals issued to refugees for 24 hrs. ending 0900 – 189. The feeding of refugees has now been stopped. Since 1st December 1919 this unit has been hard at work feeding and looking after the refugees.	S/D
	22.			S/D
	23.			
	24.			
	25.		Wagons being cleaned and painted.	
	26.		Number of patients put on Ambulance train No 3. from No 1 C.C.S. Officers {Lying 3, Sitting 4} O.Ranks {Lying 39, Sitting 117} from No. 30th C.C.S. Officers {Lying 3, Sitting –} O.Ranks {Lying 47, Sitting 14} At 3.30 p.m. a Demobilisation train of New Zealanders came in, all on board received a hot meal.	S/D
	27.			S/D
	28.		Weather dull & showery.	S/D

1/31/19.

D. To Brown Scott
OC ½ Fourth Fd. Amb.

ORGANIZATION
of
XXII CORPS HALTE REPAS
at
MONS.

On arrival of a Demobilization Train, two orderlies will at once be detailed from each coach to fall in under the Quartermaster Sergeant of the Train, and proceed to the Cookhouse on the right.

One orderly will receive a camp kettle of hot food; the other will receive bread, jam, and cheese for his coach.
This meal is an addition to the ordinary day's rations.

The remainder of the personnel in the train will line up with their Mess tins and a second receptacle or water bottle and proceed to the shed of the HALTE REPAS where they will be issued with free soup and tea.

They should proceed as quickly as possible right through the shed to their own coaches, after making any purchases they wish at the Canteen.

Camp kettles must be returned by the orderlies at the earliest possible moment to the cookhouse.

Tea and soup (without payment) will be available for Officers at the Officers Counter in the Canteen.

Latrines and urinals, as well as ablution benches with hot water, soap, towels, etc. are situated between the train and the shed of the HALTE REPAS.

WAR DIARY
or
INTELLIGENCE SUMMARY.

Army Form C. 2118.

1/2 Lowland Field Ambulance

Vol 12
140/3006

War Diary for the month of March 1919.

Vol 46

17 JUL 1919

Army Form C. 2118.

WAR DIARY
or
INTELLIGENCE SUMMARY
(Erase heading not required.)

Instructions regarding War Diaries and Intelligence Summaries are contained in F.S. Regs., Part II. and the Staff Manual respectively. Title pages will be prepared in manuscript.

Place	Date	Hour	Summary of Events and Information	Remarks and references to Appendices
Noo Pey Station	March 1919 1st		At 6 am a train load of reinforcements proceeding to the RHINE was issued with a hot meal at the Halte Repas.	S/P
	2nd		Weather - Bright	S/P
	3rd		A demobilisation train with 900 South African troops on board was issued with a hot meal.	S/P
			At 2pm a train with 400 men on board proceeding for demobilisation was given a hot meal.	S/P
	4th		A train with 800 on board proceeding to the Rhine was issued with a hot meal.	S/P
	5th		A demobilisation train with New Zealanders on board arrived at 6.30 p.m. and was issued with a hot meal.	S/P
			A train with 1100 troops proceeding to the Rhine was given a hot meal.	S/P
	6th		At 3.15 am a train with troops for demobilisation arrived & given a hot meal.	S/P

WAR DIARY
~~INTELLIGENCE SUMMARY~~

Army Form C. 2118.

(Erase heading not required.)

Instructions regarding War Diaries and Intelligence Summaries are contained in F. S. Regs., Part II. and the Staff Manual respectively. Title pages will be prepared in manuscript.

Place	Date 1919	Hour	Summary of Events and Information	Remarks and references to Appendices
Mons Rly Station	MARCH 6th		6 trains with about 900 troops going for demobilization was fed at 7.15pm.	S/p
	7th		Number of patients put on board ambce 3 train. Officers Sgrs 6 ORanks Sgrs 97 Sitting 5 Sitting 106	S/p
			Three demobilization trains were fed at the Halte Repas.	S/p
	8th		Two demobilization trains were fed at the Halte Repas.	S/p
	9th		One train with troops for the Rhine and two demobilization trains were fed at the Halte Repas.	S/p
	10th		Two demobilization trains fed at Halte Repas.	S/p
	11th		Two demobilization trains and one for the Rhine were fed at the Halte Repas.	S/p
	12th		One Reinforcement train going Eastward and two Demobilization trains were fed at the HALTE. REPAS.	COS

WAR DIARY
or
INTELLIGENCE SUMMARY.
(Erase heading not required.)

Army Form C. 2118.

Place	Date 1919	Hour	Summary of Events and Information	Remarks and references to Appendices
MONS RLY STATION.	MARCH 13		Large numbers of men going to the Army of Occupation from XXII Corps were issued with hot drinks at the Buffet on No 1 Platform. Two Demob Trains were fed at the HALTE REPAS.	C.63.
"	14 "		400. 1/7 Royal Scots. were issued with a hot meal before proceeding to the Rhine. One Canadian Demob Train and one Horse train were also fed at the HALTE REPAS.	C.63.
"	15 "		No 142. Ambulance Train was loaded with 23 lying & 22 sitting Cases from No 30 C.C.S. and 78 lying and 142. sitting Cases from No 1. C.C.S.	C.63.
"	16 "		One So. African Demob Train and two Horses trains were fed at the HALTE REPAS.	C.63.
"	17 "		Two Demobilisation trains were fed at the HALTE REPAS.	C.63.

Army Form C. 2118.

WAR DIARY
or
INTELLIGENCE SUMMARY.

(Erase heading not required.)

Instructions regarding War Diaries and Intelligence Summaries are contained in F. S. Regs., Part II. and the Staff Manual respectively. Title pages will be prepared in manuscript.

Place	Date 1919	Hour	Summary of Events and Information	Remarks and references to Appendices
MONS Ry STATION	MARCH 18		Lieut. Col. Dobson Scott M/C relinquished command of the Unit on proceeding to U.K. for Demobilisation. Capt. McDonald proceeded on a tour of inspection of HALTE. REPAS. on the way to the Base.	C102.
	19"		Two Demob trains and one east going train was fed at the HALTE. REPAS.	C102.
	20"		3 Pres trains were fed at Halte Repas	C102.
	21"		2/1st London Fd. Ambs. took over XXII Halte Repas Preparing to move	C102.
	22"		17 men attached to No.1 C.C.S. for duty. Cadre moved to SOIGNIES.	C102.
SOIGNIES	23"			
	24"			
	25"		nothing doing	C163.
	26"			
	27"			
	28"			

Army Form C. 2118.

WAR DIARY
or
INTELLIGENCE SUMMARY.
(Erase heading not required.)

Instructions regarding War Diaries and Intelligence Summaries are contained in F. S. Regs., Part II. and the Staff Manual respectively. Title pages will be prepared in manuscript.

Place	Date	Hour	Summary of Events and Information	Remarks and references to Appendices
SOIGNIES	MARCH 1919 29th 30th 31st		Weather very cold with heavy falls of snow.	903.

C.B.Stuntz — Major:
O.C. 1/2 Lowland. Field Amber. R.A.M.C (T)

Army Form C. 2118.

WAR DIARY
or
INTELLIGENCE SUMMARY.
(Erase heading not required.)

Instructions regarding War Diaries and Intelligence Summaries are contained in F. S. Regs., Part II. and the Staff Manual respectively. Title pages will be prepared in manuscript.

Place	Date	Hour	Summary of Events and Information	Remarks and references to Appendices

D. D. & L., London, E.C.
(A8004) Wt. W4771/M2 31 750,000 5/17 Sch 52 Forms/C2118/14

140/3550.

New Zealand F.A.

17 JUL 1919

Army Form C. 2118.

WAR DIARY
or
INTELLIGENCE SUMMARY
(Erase heading not required.)

Place	Date	Hour	Summary of Events and Information	Remarks and references to Appendices
SOIGNIES	April 1		NOTHING DOING	
"	2			Cas.
"	3			
"	4		The Medical Equipment of the 154th Brigade Group - 56th Bde, R.F.A. and 32nd Divl. Train R.A.S.C. was inspected by Lieut Qr Riddell and Surplus Equipment returned to No. 19 A.D.M.S.	Cas.
"	5			
"	6		Ordnance Equipment surplus to New Establishment was returned to D.A.D.O.S.	Cas.

Army Form C. 2118.

WAR DIARY
or
INTELLIGENCE SUMMARY.
(Erase heading not required.)

Instructions regarding War Diaries and Intelligence Summaries are contained in F. S. Regs., Part II. and the Staff Manual respectively. Title pages will be prepared in manuscript.

Place	Date	Hour	Summary of Events and Information	Remarks and references to Appendices
SOIGNIES	APRIL 7"			
"	8"		One Ambulance Wagon, Water Cart, G.S. Wagons, and G.S. Wagon	
"	9"		and two to New Establishment were handed over to-day.	C+62
"	10"			
"	11"		Nothing doing	C+62
"	12"			
"	13"			

Army Form C. 2118.

WAR DIARY
or
INTELLIGENCE SUMMARY.
(Erase heading not required.)

Instructions regarding War Diaries and Intelligence Summaries are contained in F. S. Regs., Part II. and the Staff Manual respectively. Title pages will be prepared in manuscript.

Place	Date	Hour	Summary of Events and Information	Remarks and references to Appendices
SOIGNIES	APRIL 14th			
"	15th		Nothing of interest to report	
"	16th			C63
"	17th			
"	18th			
"	19th			
"	20th			

Army Form C. 2118.

WAR DIARY
or
INTELLIGENCE SUMMARY.
(Erase heading not required.)

Instructions regarding War Diaries and Intelligence Summaries are contained in F. S. Regs., Part II. and the Staff Manual respectively. Title pages will be prepared in manuscript.

Place	Date	Hour	Summary of Events and Information	Remarks and references to Appendices
SOIGNIES	APRIL 22nd		Nothing of interest to report apart from usual day's routine	
"	23rd		- do -	
"	24th		- do -	
"	25th		- do -	C.63
"	26th		- do -	
"	27th		- do -	
"	28th		- do -	

Army Form C. 2118.

WAR DIARY
or
INTELLIGENCE SUMMARY.
(Erase heading not required.)

Place	Date	Hour	Summary of Events and Information	Remarks and references to Appendices
SOIGNIES	APRIL 29		Nothing of interest to report	C.52.
"	30		—do—	

C.S.Whitmajor
(A.C. Med. Law. Fd. Attica)
R.A.M. CORPS, T

No/3560

28 JUL 1919

1/2 Lowland Fd Amb
1/2 LFA Army Form C. 2118.

WAR DIARY
or
INTELLIGENCE SUMMARY
(Erase heading not required.)

Place	Date	Hour	Summary of Events and Information	Remarks and references to Appendices
Oignies	May 1		Nothing of interest to report	9/2/14
"	2		— do —	
"	3		Amendment made to Table issued with Mons Codres No. D.1573 Staff and Q.R. reduced to 1 Officer and 44 O.R. in place of 2 Officers and 44 O.R. as given in table of reduction for Field Amb. Cadres.	
"	4		Nothing of interest to report	
"	5		— do —	
"	6		— do —	
"	7		— do —	W.L.
"	8		— do —	

Army Form C. 2118.

1/2 LYA

WAR DIARY
or
INTELLIGENCE SUMMARY
(Erase heading not required.)

Instructions regarding War Diaries and Intelligence Summaries are contained in F. S. Regs., Part II. and the Staff Manual respectively. Title pages will be prepared in manuscript.

Place	Date	Hour	Summary of Events and Information	Remarks and references to Appendices
Shipmed	May 9		Nothing of interest to report	
	10		– do –	
	11		– do –	
	12		9 R.A.M.C. and 2 R.A.S.C. surplus O. Ranks on Cadre for table of 3rd inst. leave for concentration camp at Havre	
	13		Nothing of interest to report	
	14		– do –	
	15		– do –	
	16		– do –	W.L.
	17		– do –	
	18		– do –	
	19		– do –	

WAR DIARY
or
INTELLIGENCE SUMMARY.

(Erase heading not required.)

Army Form C. 2118.

Place	Date	Hour	Summary of Events and Information	Remarks and references to Appendices
Cyprus	May 20		Nothing of Interest to report	
	21		— do —	
	22		— do —	
	23		— do —	
	24		Lieut & Mrs Liddell returned from Leave to U.K.	
	25		Nothing of Interest to report	
	26		10 R.A.M.C. O.R's enlisted in 1944 sent for consideration transf. to others A.S. 212 Ufd 27/5/17	
	27		Orders to be returned by 75% of original establishment Auth. 02669	
	28		Nothing of interest to report	
	29		— do —	
	30		— do —	
	31		— do —	
			W. Liddell	
			Lieut.	

www.ingramcontent.com/pod-product-compliance
Lightning Source LLC
Chambersburg PA
CBHW081408160426
43193CB00013B/2136